Changing Patterns of
Child-bearing and
Child Rearing

Changing Patterns of Child-bearing and Child Rearing

Proceedings of the Seventeenth Annual Symposium of the Eugenics Society London 1980

Edited by

R. CHESTER
Department of Social Administration, The University, Hull, England

PETER DIGGORY
Department of Obstetrics and Gynaecology, Kingston Hospital, Kingston, Surrey, England and *Royal Marsden Hospital, Sutton, Surrey*

MARGARET B. SUTHERLAND
School of Education, University of Leeds, Leeds, England

1981

Academic Press
A Subsidiary of Harcourt Brace Jovanovich, Publishers
London · New York · Toronto · Sydney · San Francisco

ACADEMIC PRESS INC. (LONDON) LTD.
24/28 Oval Road,
London NW1

United States Edition published by
ACADEMIC PRESS INC.
111 Fifth Avenue
New York, New York 10003

British Library Cataloguing in Publication Data
Changing patterns of child bearing and child rearing.
1. Obstetrics — Congresses   2. Pediatrics — Congresses
3. Children — Care and hygiene — Congresses
I. Chester, R.   II. Diggory, P. L. C.
III. Sutherland, M. B.
618.3'2   RG31   81-67896

ISBN 0-12-171660-0

Text set in 11/12 pt Compugraphic Baskerville by Dobbie Typesetting Service, Plymouth, Devon
and Printed by T.J. Press (Padstow) Limited, Padstow, Cornwall

Contributors

EVA ALBERMAN, *Department of Clinical Epidemiology, London Hospital Medical College, Turner Street, London E1 2AD.*

R. W. BEARD, *Department of Obstetrics and Gynaecology, St. Mary's Hospital Medical School, London W2 1PG.*

N. G. BLURTON JONES, *Department of Growth and Development, Institute of Child Health, 30 Guilford Street, London WC1N 1EH.*

JACQUELINE BURGOYNE, *Faculty of Applied Social Studies, Sheffield City Polytechnic, Collegiate Crescent Site, Sheffield S10 2BP.*

IAIN CHALMERS, *National Perinatal Epidemiology Unit, Radcliffe Infirmary, Oxford OX2 6HE.*

DAVID CLARK, *MRC Medical Sociology Unit, Institute of Medical Sociology, Westburn Road, Aberdeen AB9 2ZE.*

PETER DIGGORY, *Department of Obstetrics and Gynaecology, Kingston Hospital, Kingston upon Thames* and *Royal Marsden Hospital, Sutton, Surrey.*

TONY HIPGRAVE, *School of Social Work, University of Leicester, 107 Princess Road East, Leicester LE1 7LA.*

DOUGLAS HOOPER, *Department of Social Administration, University of Hull, Hull HU6 7RX.*

ALEX MCGLAUGHLIN, *Department of Social Administration, University of Hull, Hull HU6 7RX.*

W. A. MARSHALL, *Department of Human Sciences, University of Technology, Loughborough, Leics LE11 3TU.*

J. L. PEARCE, *Department of Paediatrics, Wexham Park Hospital, Slough, Berks SL2 4HL.*

M. P. M. RICHARDS, *Child Care and Development Group, Department of Paediatrics, University of Cambridge, Free School Lane, Cambridge CB2 3RF.*

Preface

This book contains the papers presented at the seventeenth annual symposium of the Eugenics Society in September 1980. The symposium was the third of a series; the two earlier symposia had considered changing patterns of sexual behaviour and changing patterns of conception and fertility.

The present volume deals with obstetric and perinatal events, and with our understanding of (particularly early) child-rearing and its variant patterns. Within the papers there is some attention to the link between these two matters, and some emphasis on outcomes of experience at delivery and early parental behaviour, as well as consideration of certain implications for the various kinds of professionals who are involved in such affairs. The first day of the meeting, including the Galton Lecture, was devoted to the clinical scene. Readers will appreciate that on the one hand there has been a rapidly increasing use of high technology in the monitoring of labour, designed to protect the fetus, and on the other hand an increasing realization that labour is a family event, and that there are real advantages in allowing a woman to perform in a way, and in a setting, which is best suited to her personality, needs, and family relationships. There are certain tensions in this situation, some of them reflected in the papers which follow, and there is much to discuss for those who are professionally concerned with the management of childbirth.

The paucity of data concerning the effectiveness of the new technical monitoring aids, together with their high financial costs in a time of economic difficulty, calls attention to the need both for adequate trials and for discussion of priorities. In addition, the increasing introduction of this technology tends to threaten the future status of the midwife as we know her. Those who feel that these are matters of concern will find much of interest in the concept of "perinatal audit", and in the statistics provided. Furthermore, comparison with other countries together with regional and class variations in the United Kingdom show that we have not reached any irreducible limits, and indeed have far to go in providing optimal perinatal care for all.

Soon after delivery the care of the child becomes primarily the responsibility of the parent, and the second day of the Symposium was devoted largely to certain social aspects of child-rearing. Here again, however, interaction between the parent and the new-born child was shown to be affected in various ways by the clinical management at labour and early neo-natal life. In addition, attention was given to generational continuities in child-rearing practices, and to an evaluation of the contemporary child-bearing and child-rearing situations in evolutionary perspective, with some suggestion that there may not be a particularly good fit between current practices and our evolved nature. The final session drew attention to the fact that increasingly large numbers of children are not reared by two biological parents in a traditional domestic situation, and to issues concerned with the continuing existence of professionals' intervention in parenting long after birth.

Rapid changes of both the technical and social kind have made it urgently necessary to study the need for and outcomes of various types of professional intervention in parturition and parenting. All of the authors represented here are actively engaged in the work on which they write, and virtually every paper concerned the rapidity of change which is occurring. In a subject of such universal importance it is likely that there will be few who will not find new, interesting, and challenging ideas in the proceedings of the Symposium.

on behalf of the Eugenics Society
R. CHESTER
PETER DIGGORY
MARGARET B. SUTHERLAND

October, 1981

Contents

Technology in the Care of Mother and Baby: An Essential Safeguard

R. W. BEARD

*Department of Obstetrics and Gynaecology,
St. Mary's Hospital Medical School, London*

It is not unusual nowadays to hear that technology is dehumanizing childbearing. The criticism is interesting because emotive words are used—"technology" has the ring of the unfeeling while "childbearing" recalls the warm image of a happy mother and her baby. And yet, less than half a century ago, the word childbearing struck a note of fear into any woman who still had to face it. Childbearing meant pain, sometimes prolonged for days, dangerous delivery ending quite often in the disappointment of a dead baby, and worst of all, an ever-present threat to the life of the mother. Even today an anxious father will occasionally ask the obstetrician to save the mother if the choice lies between her and the baby—an echo of the days when the obstetrician and midwife could not be certain that all would go well until the birth was over. This may be contrasted with the attitudes of modern women who confidently expect a happy outcome of their pregnancy—a confidence which is largely based on the enormous improvement in the maternal and perinatal mortality figures. It is the purpose of this paper to show how improved medical care and technology have contributed to this improvement.

The Fall in Maternal and Perinatal Mortality (PNM)

Figure 1 shows the considerable fall in maternal and PN mortality. The reasons for the consistent downward trend are still not completely clear. It must be acknowledged that there has been a great improvement in the general health and the social circumstances of the general population. If this were the major cause of improvements in obstetric outcome and particularly in PNM it would be expected that the effects

1

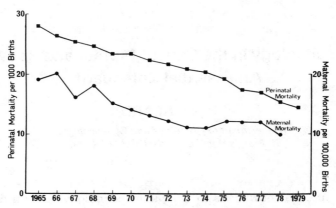

FIG. 1. Perinatal and maternal mortality in England and Wales.

would be most pronounced in social classes IV and V. However, the fall in perinatal mortality has been approximately the same in all social class groups whereas if improved socio-economic circumstances was the major cause of the fall one would have expected some equalization between the classes. Thus, it seems likely that improved systems for the care of mother and baby are likely to have played an important part in the success story. A good example of the influence of improved care on obstetric outcome is exemplified by the condition of premature separation of the placenta. This used to be a major cause of maternal death and was almost invariably fatal for the fetus. The outcome for the mother has been improved out of all recognition by the greater safety of delivery by caesarean section, the ability to correct blood clotting deficiencies, and the ready availability of blood transfusion. The prognosis for the baby that with this condition often has the added handicap of being immature, has also improved dramatically by the development of support systems that tide the baby over the first few dangerous days after delivery.

Changes in Clinical Management

As maternal mortality decreased, obstetricians were increasingly able to turn their attention towards improving the diagnosis for the fetus. In this they were assisted by the scientific investigations of workers such as Sir Joseph Barcroft, Professor of Physiology at Cambridge. Before the Second World War, his studies on unborn lambs had provided a body of information on which our present understanding of fetal life is based. Epidemiological studies by pioneers such as Sir Dugald Baird also assisted the obstetrician to identify the antecedent factors commonly associated with perinatal death. The Second Perinatal Mortality Survey (Butler and Alberman, 1969) examined all births in England and Wales during a one-week period in 1958. The results obtained had a major impact on practice as obstetricians used this information to aid their clinical decisions.

An important component of the new development in obstetric practice was the belief that if PNM could be improved, it was likely that the rate of handicap amongst the survivors would improve — an assumption that still has not been entirely proved. Two approaches for improving the welfare of the fetus were available to the obstetrician. The first, and in many ways the easiest, was that advocated by Baird (Baird and Thomson, 1969) — that is, premature delivery when it seemed that continuation of the pregnancy carried a greater risk for the fetus. This necessitated developing ''early warning systems'' which ensured that delivery was undertaken well before the fetus was damaged. This approach brought its own problems with the delivery of a baby that was sometimes so premature that it was incapable of extra-uterine survival. It is only with the advent of new technology for providing interim support for the premature baby that this problem has been resolved.

The second approach was to improve the intrauterine environment of the fetus. An example of this form of approach in treatment is the attempt to improve the condition of a growth-retarded fetus by resting the mother in hospital. The fact that there is lack of agreement amongst obstetricians on how effective this treatment is, is evidence of the need to quantify this effect with the technology now available for assessing fetal growth. There can be little doubt that in the future this approach has great potential.

Early efforts to lower PNM were not always successful. Wholesale induction of labour had little effect on PNM as is shown in Fig. 2. This shows that whilst the induction rate was increasing sharply in Britain, there was virtually no change in Norway, and yet the rate of decline of PNM was the same in both countries at that time. The desire of obstetricians to deliver babies from a potentially damaging environment was entirely understandable. However, as events proved, the disadvantages of inducing many women whose pregnancies were otherwise normal were gradually seen to outweigh the advantages.

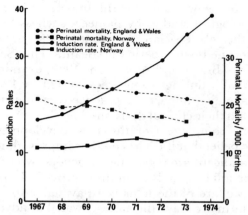

FIG. 2. The relationship between perinatal mortality and induction of labour in England and Wales, and in Norway (Chalmers and Richards, 1977).

The Development of Technological Aids

Technology has been applied increasingly in the care of the mother and baby for more than two centuries. The Chamberlayne family who practised midwifery in the seventeenth and eighteenth centuries devised a pair of forceps to overcome the problems of disproportion in which the baby was too big for the mother's pelvis. Disproportion at that time was much feared by midwives because of the high maternal and fetal mortality associated with prolonged labour. The first forceps were crude and potentially dangerous, but gradually the design was modified so that today forceps delivery carries little risk for the mother or baby (Paintin and Vincent, 1981).

Technological aids are now an essential part of maternity care. Without them, the obstetrician and paediatrician would be unable to detect and treat many of the conditions which threaten the life of the baby during pregnancy and after delivery. These "aids" play an important part in the preventive role of modern antenatal and labour care. At first sight the fact that about 95 per cent of all babies are born entirely healthy would suggest that there is not much of a problem until it is recognized that the remaining five per cent represent about 35,000 babies a year, many of whom die or, of more serious consequence, will survive with permanent handicap. Again, it would be easy if it were possible to predict at an early stage of pregnancy those mothers who were going to give birth to one of the babies from this five per cent group, but unfortunately it is not the case. All mothers are at risk of having a compromised baby, admittedly some more than others, until their baby is lying in the cot with "all systems functioning".

Table I

Summary of technological advances currently applied in the management of pregnancy

Technology	Application
Before Labour	*Before Labour*
1. Amniocentesis (puncture of the uterus for the collection of amniotic fluid).	— detection of numerous abnormalities such as hydrocephaly and mongolism.
	— assessment of maturity of fetal lungs.
	— assessment of rhesus disease.
2. Fetoscopy (transuterine telescopic visualization of the fetus).	— investigation of thalassemia.
	— detection of fetal abnormality.
3. Ultrasound (use of reflected sound waves to outline the contents of the uterus).	— assessment of age of fetus, of fetal growth, of number of fetuses, of situation of placenta in uterus, etc.
4. Fetal heart rate monitoring (continuous recording electronically of the rate).	— assessment of fetal well-being.
5. Hormone measurement in blood of mother.	— assessment of function of placenta and fetal well-being.
During Labour	*During Labour*
1. Fetal heart rate monitoring (as above).	— assessment of fetal well-being.
2. Fetal blood sampling and measurement of pH.	— diagnostic test for fetal asphyxia.
3. Measurement of uterine activity.	— assessment and regulation of normal uterine activity.
After Delivery	*After Delivery*
Neonatal Intensive Care — Examples	
Continuous measurement of oxygenation.	— Assessment of condition of newborn.
Recording of respiratory rate.	
Ultrasound visualization of brain.	
Continuous positive airway pressure (CPAP).	— Respiratory support.

Table I summarizes some of the more important of the technological advances that have proved to be of real value and which are now in regular use. These measures have been divided into the stage of pregnancy when they are employed. They can also be subdivided

condition of the fetus, diagnosis of asphyxia was often made relatively late, leading occasionally to the death of the fetus (Beard, 1968).

A significant advance in assessing the condition of the fetus came with the introduction of fetal blood sampling during labour (Saling, 1962). In this technique a metal tube is passed up the vagina and through the cervix (neck of the womb) so that the head of the baby is visualized. A small prick is then made in the fetal scalp and a very small volume of blood collected in a fine capillary tube. The acidity of this blood (pH), which is a reliable measure of tissue asphyxia, can then be measured. As the degree of asphyxia increases, the acidity also becomes more pronounced and the pH falls. If the pH is 7.30 or above, it can reasonably be assumed that the fetus is well-oxygenated. Below this figure asphyxia is suspected and at levels below 7.25 a definite diagnosis can be made, particularly in conjunction with other forms of monitoring.

Initially, fetal blood sampling was used in conjunction with other diagnostic techniques such as auscultation. It is now also used as a means of determining the significance of an abnormal trace obtained by electronic recording of the continuous fetal heart rate. A trace is obtained by attaching a small electrode to the head of the fetus, the lead passing through the cervix and transmitting the signal from each heart beat directly (or, more recently, by radio-telemetry) to a small computer. This analyses the signal to produce an instantaneous rate. Figure 3 shows a normal trace. The early pioneers who developed this system were only seeking a continuous record of the FHR, but subsequent research revealed that there was a great deal more information to be obtained from the trace. For instance, the variability or fluctuations of the trace are a function of the cardiac reflexes which regulate the activity of the heart. The more asphyxiated the fetus, the less the variability of the trace. Another useful feature is the relationship of the "slowing" (or "deceleration") to the contraction. In Fig. 4, which is a trace from an asphyxiated fetus, the interval between the lowest point of the deceleration and the peak of the contraction is about 30–40 seconds which is a feature of moderate or severe fetal asphyxia.

Electronic fetal heart rate monitoring provides a good deal more information than auscultation but it cannot tell the obstetrician whether changes in the fetal heart rate are due to factors other than asphyxia, such as the drugs used for pain relief in labour, or the compression of the fetal head as it passes down the birth canal. Here, the use of fetal blood sampling in conjunction with fetal heart rate

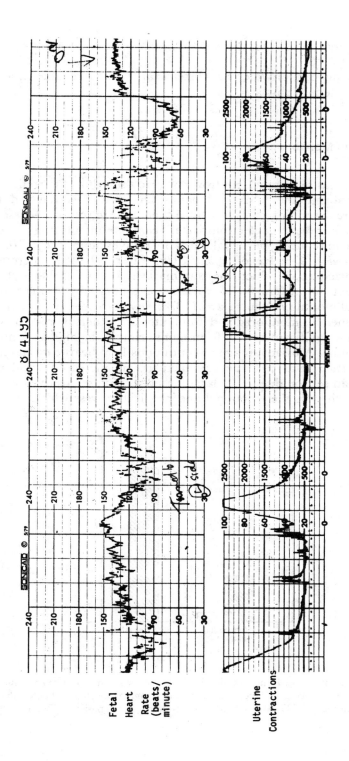

Fetal
Heart
Rate
(beats/
minute)

Uterine
Contractions

Fig. 4. Fetal heart rate trace showing late decelerations.

monitoring can provide the obstetrician with a reliable system for detecting fetal asphyxia.

Results of Monitoring

There has been much controversy as to the value of current systems of monitoring the fetus in labour. The reader is referred to the literature describing trials that have been done to resolve the issue as to whether intrapartum electronic fetal heart rate monitoring has proved effective in reducing perinatal mortality (Haverkamp *et al.*, 1976, 1979; Kelso *et al.*, 1978; Renou *et al.*, 1976; Parer, 1979). Numerous non-randomized trials which are summarized in Fig. 5 have shown a consistent improvement of variable amounts in intrapartum and neonatal mortality. Neutra *et al.* (1978), in a retrospective trial in which he matched his monitored and unmonitored mothers by risk categories, showed a significant benefit from monitoring in the high and moderate risk groups. A disadvantage of continuous fetal heart rate monitoring *used without* fetal pH measurement is an increased incidence of caesarean section due to the large numbers of false positive diagnoses. Finally, there is the emotional and physical distress which may result

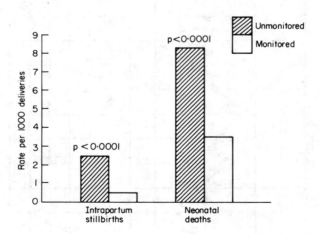

FIG. 5. A summary of 10 non-randomized trials showing the effect of continuous fetal heart rate monitoring in labour on fetal and neonatal mortality. Pooled data from monitored (37,733 patients) and unmonitored (73,774 patients) (Parer, 1979).

from being attached to a monitor throughout labour. This is difficult to quantify but clearly needs serious attention.

Unfortunately, much of the discussion about the contribution of technology to the welfare of the mother and her baby has tended to centre around the relative merits of fetal monitoring during labour, and has resulted in the emergence of two groups with conflicting objectives. On the one hand, there are those, mostly obstetricians, whose main objective is to ensure the safety of the fetus, while on the other hand there is the group that believes there is a danger that the whole sequence of events leading to the birth of a baby, in which the mother takes pleasure, will be interfered with. Both groups tend to overstate their case: those in favour claim that the benefit of monitoring requires no further demonstration, whilst those against demand more rigorous trials than it is possible to do before monitoring can be accepted.

The reality of the situation is that existing fetal monitoring systems are an improvement on the old method of auscultation but they require thorough education of the staff who use them. A thorough explanation to mothers in the antenatal period about monitoring techniques and the added safety for their babies is obviously essential. Improvements in the design of monitors and the search for more precise diagnostic systems is also an important objective.

In summary, technology has made a valuable contribution to improving the obstetrician's insight into the well-being of the fetus. Probably the most important development for the future is that he should learn to use these new tools effectively.

References

Baird, D. and Thomson, A. M. (1969). Reduction of perinatal mortality by improving standards of obstetric care. In *Perinatal Problems: The Second Report of the 1958 British Perinatal Mortality Survey*, edited by N. R. Butler and E. D. Alberman, pp. 255–282. Edinburgh and London: Churchill Livingstone.

Beard, R. W. (1968). The effect of fetal blood sampling on caesarean section for fetal distress. *Journal of Obstetrics and Gynaecology of the British Commonwealth*, **75**, 1291–1295.

Butler, N. R. and Alberman, E. D. (Editors) (1969). *Perinatal Problems: The Second Report of the 1958 British Perinatal Mortality Survey*. Edinburgh and London: Churchill Livingstone.

Chalmers, I. and Richards, M. (1977). Intervention and causal inference in obstetric practice. In *Benefits and Hazards of the New Obstetrics*, edited by T. Chard and M. P. M. Richards, pp. 34–61. Clinics in Developmental Medicine, No. 64. London: Spastics International Medical Publications/Heinemann Medical Books.

Haverkamp, A. D., Thompson, H. E., McFee, J. G. and Cetrulo, C. (1976). The evaluation of continuous fetal heart rate monitoring in high risk pregnancy. *American Journal of Obstetrics and Gynecology*, **125**, 310–320.

Haverkamp, A. D., Orleans, M., Langendoerfer, S., McFee, J. G., Murphy, J. and Thompson, H. E. (1979). A controlled trial of the differential effects of intrapartum fetal monitoring. *American Journal of Obstetrics and Gynecology*, **134**, 399–412.

Kelso, I. M., Parsons, R. J., Lawrence, F. G., Arora, S. S., Edmonds, D. K. and Cooke, I. D. (1978). An assessment of continuous fetal heart rate monitoring in labor: a randomized trial. *American Journal of Obstetrics and Gynecology*, **131**, 526–532.

Neutra, R. R., Fienburg, S. E., Greenland, S. and Friedman, E. A. (1978). Effect of fetal monitoring on neonatal death rates. *New England Journal of Medicine*, **299**, 324–326.

Paintin, D. B. and Vincent, F. (1981). Forceps delivery — obstetric outcome. In *Outcomes of Obstetric Intervention in Britain*. Edited by R. W. Beard and D. B. Paintin. Proceedings of the Scientific Meeting of the Royal College of Obstetricians and Gynaecologists, May 1980. (In press)

Parer, J. T. (1979). Fetal heart rate monitoring. *Lancet*, *ii*, 632–633.

Renou, P., Chang, A., Anderson, I. and Wood, C. (1976). Controlled trial of fetal intensive care. *American Journal of Obstetrics and Gynecology*, **126**, 470–476.

Saling, E. (1962). Neues Vorgehen zur Untersuchung des Kindes unter der Geburt. *Archiv für Gynäkologie*, **197**, 108–122.

Care of the Premature Baby:
Needs and Prospects

J. L. PEARCE

Wexham Park Hospital,
Slough, Berkshire

Nowadays our standards of perinatal care are judged more and more by statistics. The perinatal mortality rate, that is the number of deaths from 28 weeks pregnant up to and including the first week of life, has roughly halved in the last 15 years. Many of us would like to claim responsibility but the reasons for this improvement are multifactorial. Better care of the baby contributes only a small but significant share to the lower mortality figures. As the majority of baby deaths occur in low birth-weight babies, I will consider some aspects of the modern management of this group.

Let us follow the course of a fictitious pregnancy of about 28 weeks. The pregnant lady feels some twinges in the lower abdomen and realizes that she is in premature labour. We will hope that in this case antenatal care has succeeded in teaching her to recognize the symptoms of premature labour and to be aware of the extreme urgency of the occurrence.

She is admitted and the diagnosis of premature labour confirmed, not always easily done. In the far-sighted maternity hospital an obstetric and paediatric consultant should now be involved in the management. One of the more important decisions the two consultants from a smaller unit will now make is where the pregnant mother should continue to be managed. Should she be transferred to a regional centre or managed locally? The advent of the regional centre may represent one of the most significant advances in perinatal care in the last decade. These centres have succeeded in concentrating obstetric and neonatal expertise and in many areas offer a superbly organized referral service.

With the advent of regional centres, a whole new science of transport techniques for small babies, usually in ambulance or aircraft, has developed. In recent years, however, we have had finally to admit that no amount of sophisticated equipment can compete with the most advanced transport incubator of all, that is, the mother's uterus. Transfer of the mother before birth, if there is time, with delivery at the referral centre, has become popular (Merenstein *et al.*, 1977; Blake and Pollitzer, 1979). Overall, the decision to transfer is an individual one, with many factors that must be considered. Let us return to our 28-weeker and pretend that a local delivery was favoured in this case.

We now enter what should be one of the most exciting areas in perinatal medicine, namely, the arrest of premature labour (Wynn and Wynn, 1977). What a challenge for obstetricians, the chance to silence neonatal paediatricians once and for all by doing them out of a job. The prevention of pre-term delivery would reduce the perinatal mortality rate and shut Special Care baby units all over the country. Think what funds could be re-directed into other branches of obstetrics. Unfortunately the scientific evidence is not yet before us, and clinical trials have so far failed to give a clear message (Hemminki and Starfield, 1978; *British Medical Journal*, 1979). Suffice it to say that, with favourable circumstances, in many hospitals some attempt would be made to arrest the labour, usually with intravenous beta sympathomimetic drugs or alcohol.

At the same time the labouring mother may well receive an injection of betamethasone into her thigh. Liggins and Howie published in 1972 the original and, in my opinion, the best study on the use of steroids to prevent the dreaded respiratory distress syndrome. This was the main cause of death of premature babies. Their figures, up-dated in 1978, showed that between 30 and 32 weeks gestation, steroids for longer than 24 h would virtually prevent respiratory distress syndrome (Howie and Liggins, 1978). Only 2 babies out of 23 mothers treated developed the disease as opposed to 14 out of 25 in the controls. The results at other gestation ages below 34 weeks were less impressive but just made statistical significance.

Others have confirmed their findings that betamethasone should not be given to toxaemic mothers. It is also suggested that with membranes ruptured for longer than 48 h the chances of respiratory distress syndrome anyway are very small (Thibeault and Emmanouilides, 1977). Let us imagine that our good lady, whose bed rest alone has a 50:50 chance of inhibiting her labour, inexorably progresses. All too often she will stop and start, and despite arrays of monitoring equipment, and with apologies to the obstetricians, she will confound us all by quietly delivering in the bed. Her actual delivery and then reception by the paediatric team should point to another major advance. It is now realized that senior obstetric and paediatric staff are needed to manage what may be one of the most dangerous 30 minutes of the next 70 years of that individual's life. The aims of the attendant are to maintain the circulation which usually means maintaining the heart beat, and to prevent asphyxia, if necessary by intubation.

A breathing, warm and peaceful baby should be delivered to the Special Care baby unit which takes over the responsibility of the uterus. Gradually, however, the baby's breathing rate increases and at first a low moan becomes a grunt. He is developing the respiratory distress syndrome. The very name strikes fear in the hearts of the paediatric staff. It is 50 years since Van Naergaard (1929) postulated the existence of a factor that lowers surface tension in the lung. Clements et al. (1958) elucidated the physical properties of what is now known as surfactant and Avery and Mead (1959) showed that lungs of babies dying of respiratory distress syndrome did not contain it. Gluck and others (1971) defined its phospholipid structure and opened the way for the lecithin–sphyngomyelin ratio to detect the lung maturity of the fetus.

The most exciting question of all is, can we administer surfactant postnatally? Some success has been achieved in the experimental animal and in January of this year (1980), Fujiwara and colleagues from Japan reported success in treating ten babies with severe respiratory distress syndrome. They cured the breathing disease by depositing a mixture of synthetic and natural surfactant down endotracheal tubes into the baby's lungs.

On the more clinical front, the advance in the management of respiratory failure in very small babies has led to the Intensive Care set-ups we now associate with Special Care baby units. There is little wonder that the rights of mother and baby can be lost altogether beneath the weight of clinical expertise and the plethora of scientific equipment. Undoubtedly ventilation of the sick, tiny baby represents the pinnacle of neonatal work. We will not review the precise methodology or advances in ventilator design that are familiar to those working in the field.

Another advance in the treatment of the respiratory distress syndrome occurred when Harrison in South Africa asked the simple question — why do babies grunt in this disorder? (Harrison et al., 1968). He showed that when the grunt was abolished by intubation the baby's blood oxygen fell. It seemed then quite natural to put the grunt back or increase it by placing a resistance on the baby's out-flow breathing circuit. Gregory, as far back as 1971, published his classic trial on what is known in the trade as C.P.A.P., or continuous positive airway pressure (Gregory et al., 1971). He demonstrated an impressive rise in oxygen tension when a resistance was applied. How those little babies must have rued the day. Since then we have encased their heads in helmets and plastic bags, pressed masks on their faces and stuck tubes up their little noses.

With all these advances it became even more important to monitor the oxygen in the blood of the premature baby. It took about 30 to 40 years after oxygen was introduced for premature babies for us to decide that too much oxygen tension in the blood causes retrolental fibroplasia, a form of blindness. Then, a few years after that, being too cautious with oxygen caused brain damage. We therefore walk a tightrope in neonatal intensive care, between too much or too little. The ability to measure gas pressure and pH in blood opened up ever-increasingly sophisticated methods of oxygen monitoring. Usually blood has to be collected from heel pricks, catheters in the umbilical artery, and direct needle puncture of arteries. A team from University College Hospital then produced an oxygen probe neatly placed at the end of the umbilical catheter so that for the first time a constant record of the baby's oxygen tension could be monitored. Probes that measure the oxygen saturation of haemoglobin have also been developed.

A major advance, however, which puts neonatal medicine into the brave new scientific world has been the development of the transcutaneous oxygen monitor. The small electrode warms the skin to increase blood flow and allows molecules of oxygen to diffuse across a semi-permeable membrane into an electro-chemical compartment. Machines that can measure carbon dioxide and anaesthetic gases as well will soon be commercially available. This surely will herald the era of armchair neonatal intensive care. The supreme advantage, of course, is that the interference with the baby is kept to a minimum. Even slight interference, such as handling, nappy changes, etc. may produce critical falls in blood oxygen tension. In the sick baby a slight change in the ventilator setting may produce dramatic improvement. Of course, there are still problems with the apparatus and it does not do to ask how much it costs.

Our baby, obviously unimpressed by his scientific environment, now has a brief series of contractions of his limbs, interpreted as a convulsion. Part of the work-up may include an ultrasound scan of his brain (Pape et al., 1979). We are familiar with its use in obstetrics. The development of this tool for outlining the anatomy of the human body by using echoes from high frequency waves has come a long way from the squeaks of the vampire bat but has the same principle. The ultrasound beam is transmitted through the baby's anterior fontanelle. The anatomy of the brain can be demonstrated almost as clearly as the CAT* scan without irradiation. The lateral ventricles of the brain and

*Computerized Axial Tomography

the septum pellucidum can be clearly seen. We can detect such conditions as intracranial haemorrhage or hydrocephalus. The size and position of the haemorrhage already give us information about the outlook for the baby. This also gives the impetus for research to prevent intracranial haemorrhage and to minimize its effect.

Our little baby now turns the corner to recover and starts to be fed. Although less dramatic, the methods available for feeding small babies have quietly progressed. Intragastric, intrajejunal and intravenous feeding all have an established place. After initial controversy, most units now use expressed breast milk, preferably from the baby's own mother. Even the ability of low birth-weight babies to actually suckle at the breast has been rediscovered (Pearce and Buchanan, 1979). Our enthusiasm for breast milk has led to the setting-up of breast milk banks. Expressed breast milk is frozen and gathered from breast-feeding mothers in the community. A sample is cultured, the remainder banked, pasteurized if necessary, thawed and fed to these tiny babies. Breast milk is, indeed, a biological fluid. The list of immunological properties grows with each reviewer. We now know the constituents of breast milk vary from woman to woman, from feed to feed, throughout the same feed as well as the stage of lactation (Hytten, 1954). Even the mother who has a premature baby secretes milk richer in protein, i.e. more attuned to her little baby than to a full-term one (Gross et al., 1980). A plethora of scientific literature is available about the benefits of human milk, as much a tribute to the female breast as to the ingenuity of man who has documented it!

Another interesting change has also come about in Special Care baby units by the appreciation of the bond between mother, family and baby. What an example of the circular process of so-called scientific progress! Just as the enthusiasm for specialized care of babies gained momentum, an equal and opposite reaction suggested that babies should remain with their mothers and be kept out of Special Care baby units (Brimblecombe et al., 1978). The process of bonding between mother and baby has undoubtedly become a bandwagon in recent years, possibly because many hospital personnel had to be educated by lay people, mostly mothers, about the need for baby contact. The result has been that the admission rate has been drastically reduced in many units, the doors thrown open to visitors, and even the hallowed gowns and other apparel abandoned. There has been a welcoming of parents, grandparents and the worst terror of all, other children. Mothers are encouraged to look after their own babies even to the extent of tube feeding. In many units, bedrooms are provided for the mothers to stay, and some of the rooms are even free of hospital paint, linoleum and smell.

It is hoped that these factors, together with early discharge from hospital, have considerably improved the lot of the premature baby and his family.

What of the future of the care of the premature baby? Development of Special Care baby units depends on the birth rate and other un-predictables. A falling birth rate may reduce the need for these units especially when combined with a lower admission rate, early discharge and transfer of very small babies to regional centres. It seems likely that from an efficiency standpoint only large maternity units will be built, possibly with not less than 3,000 births per year. Many mothers, however, want the Cottage Hospital touch, with roses round the door and the individual attention that is often lacking in the big place. Furthermore, the "small is beautiful" people claim that the larger centres justify their existence by treating the complications they cause by their interference in the first place. And we would have a spirited discussion if the question of home deliveries was also raised. It seems strange to me that we cannot combine smaller and more personal units within a larger complex and that we cannot seem to de-hospitalize maternity units. Everybody seems to agree with this principle but in reality we are still offered package deal plans for new hospitals that duplicate the faults of existing ones.

As far as regional organization of neonatal care is concerned, I would like to see less inward and more outward looking. Un-fortunately, such has been the delay in the development of regional neonatal centres that there has been little time to achieve the more important work, namely the organization of perinatal care in the other hospitals in the regions. After all, there is little point in caring superbly for a one-pound baby in the regional centre when a five or six pound baby suffers brain damage from asphyxia because of a lack of care in a hospital a few miles down the road. However, there are still very few full-time neonatologists who could be asked to organize this work.

Another question that concerns us all is the cost of neonatal care. Given a certain amount of money for health, how does this care rate in a cost-efficiency study? Few would disagree that reducing brain damage makes economic sense but what of the millions spent on keeping tiny babies alive? An increasing proportion of the regional centres' admission is concerned with an ever-decreasing size of the baby. A recent report from Australia showed that about 40% of babies weighing between 500 and 701 grams survived, that is babies of about 1–1½ lbs of birth-weight (Yu and Hollingsworth, 1980). The numbers are very small but how many months of costly intensive care were entailed? The outcome for these babies may be reviewed later. On the plus side, of course, the expertise generated by the care of these tiny babies makes what looked like a problem a few years before seem very simple now.

What of development on the shop floor, so to speak? It seems likely that the mechanism of premature labour will be worked out and in many cases prevented. As confidence in neonatal care increases, a large number of very small babies at risk *in utero* will be delivered by caesarean section to prevent trauma to the brain. It also seems likely that respiratory distress syndrome will be finally eradicated. The incidence has considerably declined latterly with improved obstetric and neonatal care anyway.

One of the most critical problems that we all face is, of course, the question of staffing of Special Care baby units, both at doctor and nursing levels. Unless more resources are available to pay more staff, and unless the status of neonatal nursing in the country is better recognized, it may be that the lack of trained staff will limit the care of premature babies more than any other factor.

In research, prevention would dominate the market. I would strongly support research into the causes of unexplained still-births which still account for too great a share of the perinatal mortality rate. An accurate test of placental function and gestational age is also needed. The initiation and inhibition of premature labour we have discussed already. Finally, still more work is needed on the precise value of fetal heart monitoring in labour.

Research is also urgently needed into the causes of congenital abnormality, particularly spina bifida and Down's syndrome. In the former respect, Professor Smithells' preliminary work on the use of multivitamins to prevent spina bifida has produced some encouraging results so far (Smithells *et al.*, 1980).

We have touched lightly on various aspects of the needs of the premature baby and future prospects. I would like to finish by emphasizing what is entirely obvious, that the aim of good perinatal care is to produce normal, well-integrated children and adults. How successful we have been in this respect will be examined in the next chapter.

References

Avery, M. E. and Mead, J. (1959). Surface properties in relation to atelectasis and hyaline membrane disease. *American Journal of Diseases of Children*, **97**, 517–523.

Blake, A. M. and Pollitzer, M. J. (1979). Referral of mothers and infants for intensive care. *British Medical Journal*, ii, 414–416.

Brimblecombe, F. S. W., Richards, M. P. M. and Roberton, N. C. R. (1978). *Separation and Special-Care Baby Units*. Clinics in Developmental Medicine, No. 68. London: Spastics International Medical Publications/Heinemann Medical Books.

British Medical Journal (1979). Editorial: Drugs in threatened pre-term labour. i, 71.

Clements, J. A., Brown, E. S. and Johnson, R. P. (1958). Pulmonary surface tension and the mucus lining of the lung: some theoretical considerations. *Journal of Applied Physiology*, 12, 262–268.

Fujiwara, T., Maeta, H., Chida, S., Morita, T., Watabe, Y. and Abe, T. (1980). Artificial surfactant therapy in hyaline-membrane disease. *Lancet*, i, 55–59.

Gluck, L., Kulovich, M. V., Borer, R. C., Brenner, P. H., Anderson, G. G. and Spellacy, W. N. (1971). Diagnosis of the respiratory stress syndrome by amniocentesis. *American Journal of Obstetrics and Gynecology*, 109, 440–445.

Gregory, G. A., Kitterman, J. A., Phibbs, R. H., Tooley, W. H. and Hamilton, W. K. (1971). Treatment of the ideopathic respiratory-distress syndrome with continuous positive airway pressure. *New England Journal of Medicine*, 284, 1333–1340.

Gross, S. J., David, R. J., Bauman, L. and Tomarelli, R. M. (1980). Nutritional composition of milk produced by the mother pre-term. *Journal of Pediatrics*, 96, 641–644.

Harrison, V. C., Hease, H. de V. and Klein, M. (1968). The significance of grunting in hyaline membrane disease. *Pediatrics*, 41, 549–559.

Hemminki, E. and Starfield, B. (1978). Prevention and treatment of premature labour by drugs: review of controlled clinical trials. *British Journal of Obstetrics and Gynaecology*, 85, 411–417.

Howie, R. N. and Liggins, G. C. (1978). Clinical trial of antepartum betamethasone therapy for prevention of respiratory distress in pre-term infants. In *Preterm Labour*. Edited by A. Anderson, R. Beard, J. M. Bridenell and P. M. Dunn, pp. 281–289. London: Royal College of Obstetricians and Gynaecologists.

Hytten, F. E. (1954). Clinical and chemical studies in human lactation — variation in major constituents during a feeding. *British Medical Journal*, i, 176–179.

Liggins, G. C. and Howie, R. N. (1972). A controlled trial of antepartum glucocorticoid treatment for prevention of the respiratory distress syndrome in premature infants. *Pediatrics*, 50, 515–525.

Merenstein, G. B., Pettett, G., Woodall, J. and Hill, J. M. (1977). An analysis of air transport results in the sick newborn. II. Antenatal and neonatal referrals. *American Journal of Obstetrics and Gynecology*, 128, 520–525.

Pape, K. E., Blackwell, R. J., Cusick, G., Sherwood, A., Houang, M. T. V., Thorburn, R. J. and Reynolds, E. O. R. (1979). Ultrasound detection of brain damage in preterm infants. *Lancet*, i, 1261–1264.

Pearce, J. L. and Buchanan, L. F. (1979). Breast milk and breast feeding in very low birthweight infants. *Archives of Diseases in Childhood*, 54, 897–898.

Smithells, R. W., Sheppard, S., Schorah, C. J., Seller, M. J., Nevin, N. C., Harris, R., Read, A. P. and Fielding, D. W. (1980). Possible prevention of neural-tube defects by preconceptional vitamin supplementation. *Lancet*, i, 339–340.

Thibeault, D. W. and Emmanouilides, G. C. (1977). Prolonged rupture of fetal membranes and decreased frequency of respiratory distress syndrome and patent ductus arteriosus in preterm infants. *American Journal of Obstetrics and Gynecology*, 129, 43–46.

Van Naergaard, K. (1929). Neue Auffassungen über einen Grundbegriff der Atem-mechanik. *Zeitschrift für die Gesamte Experimentelle Medizin*, **66**, 373.

Wynn, M. and Wynn, A. (1977). *The Prevention of Preterm Births*. London: Foundation for Education and Research in Child-Bearing.

Yu, V. Y. H. and Hollingsworth, E. (1980). Improved prognosis for infants weighing 1000 g. or less at birth. *Archives of Diseases in Childhood*, **55**, 422–426.

The Long-Term Effects upon the Child of Perinatal Events

PETER DIGGORY

Department of Obstetrics and Gynaecology,
Kingston Hospital, Kingston-upon-Thames
and
Royal Marsden Hospital, Sutton, Surrey

Galton, one of the most numerate of men, established his reputation and founded the science of Eugenics by correlating causes and their effects. In attempting to decide which perinatal events produce long-term results we are following in his footsteps.

In pregnancy, labour and in caring for the new-born, we now collect a great deal of data but we lack a co-ordinating system for follow-up and correlation. We have not yet developed adequate techniques for testing even the immediate effects of some of our obstetrics procedures. Those who came hoping to hear how a particular facet of obstetric management is associated with some definable long-term result will be disappointed. My message is that we urgently need to establish facilities which will enable us to assess the effects of our actions and thereby plan logically for the future. At present we are bemused by our technology and confused by our ethical uncertainties to such an extent that we have largely abandoned scientific methodology. As a result the value of much current clinical practice is unproven and as doctors we should seek the reasons why we are in this confused and uncertain state.

The whole management of pregnancy, labour and care of the new-born has changed dramatically and rapidly. The role of obstetricians and paediatricians has expanded and altered both in the way in which they share responsibilities between the two specialities, and in their joint extended role in reproductive care. Some of the energy which should have gone into forward planning may well have been expended in establishing our new relative status. In 1927 when the first reliable survey (Huntingford, 1978) was made only 15 per cent of deliveries took place in hospitals or maternity homes; after the war, in 1946 a second survey showed the proportion had risen to 54 per cent and now more than 99 per cent of women deliver in hospital, the vast majority under the care of a consultant obstetrician, the new-born infant being under the care of a consultant paediatrician. With joint recognition of the need to make more accurate assessments, and with co-operation between the two specialities, it should in future be relatively easy to correlate events in pregnancy, labour and early life with later development of the child. When we do so we shall be able to plan more logically to the benefit of all.

Women now have the ability to control their own fertility by contraception or, if that fails, by abortion, and by the increasing use of sterilization for themselves or for their husbands. Obstetricians notice the great change which this has produced, because in the past when a pregnant woman was first seen her feelings about being pregnant were often ambivalent. Nowadays almost every pregnant woman intended to be, and enjoys, being pregnant and is looking forward to bearing a healthy child. What she wants from her obstetrician is help and advice to that end.

The whole reproductive process has been influenced and improved by two major features. The first, and most important, is the improved general health and stature of women and their better nutrition and hygiene in pregnancy. The second is improvement in medical care.

Maternal mortality* has fallen dramatically and Professor Alberman (1977) has commented that the fall over the thirty years from 1943, when it was 184 per 100,000 to 1973 when the figure had fallen to 11 per 100,000 is possibly the best documented effect of improved medical care on record. Nowadays a woman in England and Wales is about five times more likely to be murdered than she is to die in childbirth (Home Office, 1978).

We shall be hearing a great deal about the gratifying fall in perinatal mortality. Obstetricians and paediatricians tend to assume that such improvements must have resulted from those changes in clinical practice which have been taking place over the same time span. The recent Short Report (House of Commons, 1980) called attention to the variations in perinatal mortality in different areas and quoted the 1977 figures with extremes of 10.2 per thousand births for Kingston and Richmond compared with 26.6 for Rochdale. Such comparisons are extremely misleading unless we realize that the closest and most direct correlation of perinatal mortality is with social class. In 1976 social

*Maternal mortality is defined as the number of women who die from causes associated with, or aggravated by, pregnancy per 100,000 live births.

class 1 mothers averaged a perinatal mortality of 12.7 whereas in social class V there were 24.9 deaths per thousand births (Davies, 1980). If we wish to compare the performance of one hospital with another we must make allowances for the social structure of the population under consideration.

We know that lower social class is associated with a large number of adverse factors such as increased rate of low birth-weight babies, multiple pregnancy and fetal abnormality (Illingworth, 1979). We ought to be concentrating research effort upon trying to find the reasons for these associations.

Numerous surveys have shown that single mothers are more liable to lose their babies at or around birth than are married women. In the 1970 Perinatal Survey (Chamberlain *et al.*, 1975) single women are shown to be seven times as likely to do so. In a recent survey (Macfarlane, 1980) of cerebral palsy undertaken in the Oxford region special attention was paid to babies of very low birth-weight, less than 1,500 grams at birth. Single mothers were six times as frequent in this group as in the control group of babies born in the same region and time but weighing more than 1,500 grams at birth. An illegitimate birth suggests that the mother was unsupported during pregnancy and that this lack of support may be an important factor in reproductive performance. In fact many unmarried mothers are living in stable unions, presumably enjoying financial and emotional support. The perinatal mortality rate for illegitimate births is about 40% higher than that for legitimate births. However there is a suggestion from unpublished analyses that the rate when both parents jointly register the illegitimate birth, suggesting that they may well be living in stable union, is very little higher than that for legitimate births. On the other hand the rate where the mother registers the birth on her own is much higher. This suggests that the truly unsupported unmarried mother has an even worse performance than our illegitimacy figures suggest. We do not know why this association occurs and we need research to find out (Macfarlane, 1979).

High-powered technology has radically altered our management of late pregnancy, of labour and of our care of the new-born child; particularly the premature baby. Alongside these new but controversial techniques, and over the same time span, there have been other developments which have undoubtedly contributed to improved perinatal mortality and the better health of babies now born. For example, the early detection of fetal abnormality, allowing the choice of abortion; our increased vigilance against potentially harmful drugs and against unnecessary X-rays in pregnancy; our role as educators encouraging young women to be inoculated against rubella before pregnancy, and to give up smoking at latest when they find themselves pregnant: these and the improved health of pregnant women in general all contribute. It would be invaluable if we knew just what degree of importance to allocate to each.

Although obstetricians are more vigilant nowadays in avoiding unnecessary and potentially dangerous drugs in pregnancy, some of the drugs used to inhibit the onset of premature labour (Anderson, 1979) as well as drugs and techniques used in the intensive care of low birth-weight babies have yet to be proved free of long-term ill effects (Jones *et al.*, 1979).

Big strides have been made in our understanding of fetal growth and of the complex and inter-dependent physiological changes which take place at birth. This enlarged knowledge of the normal has enabled us to appreciate variations from it and sometimes to attempt treatment where previously we should not have realized that anything was wrong.

We now possess techniques and instruments which make it possible to monitor fetal growth and function and to detect variations from normal earlier and more accurately than could ever be done by clinical methods. For example, errors in the dating of pregnancy can be avoided by an ultra-sound scan in early pregnancy. A twin pregnancy can hardly be missed if such a technique is available. It is also far more accurate than the most experienced clinician in assessing continued satisfactory fetal growth — a matter of great importance and much subject to error in the past.

With the sophisticated tools now being placed in our hands we can follow accurately numerous parameters of fetal and new-born behaviour not previously detectable. Difficulties start when we have to decide whether, in a particular case, a variation from the usual is or is not within normal limits. When unquestionably abnormal patterns emerge, we have to try and decide what is the likely cause and thus how best to treat it.

The time-lag between research and development has shortened and so obstetricians are suddenly being presented with new machines providing a wealth of information about fetal function, some of which, but not necessarily all, is clearly relevant and important. Our scientific colleagues are still uncertain about the validity and exact significance of much of this new data and it is now the practising obstetrician, whose training has in no way prepared him for the task, who must arbitrate upon which facets to accept as valid and so use them in clinical management and which to reject as for the time being unproven.

These technological developments are changing the whole practice of obstetrics and they demand of obstetricians that they change their skills and perhaps even their temperaments. In the past, obstetrics attracted doctors who enjoyed using manipulative and surgical skills and who also enjoyed the close contact and rapport they could establish with pregnant and labouring women. Possibly the speciality did not attract the most intellectual or scientific of the profession.

Training used to prepare the obstetrician to cope quickly with any emergency. Now his proper task is to predict and avoid emergencies. Most are being forced to re-read physiology, pharmacology and bio-chemistry, as well as trying to attain some slight competence in statistics — simply in order to understand the new techniques available. If some women feel that obstetrics is becoming too scientific and too remote from the labouring woman, may I assure them that most obstetricians share their view.

A perinatal event is something which happens to a fetus of more than 28 weeks' maturity, either during labour or in the first seven days of life. Good antenatal care may contribute to the fetus starting labour fitter and it may help to avoid the onset of spontaneous premature labour which is itself an important factor in perinatal morbidity and mortality.

During pregnancy the obstetrician is constantly asking himself, "Is this woman well and is her fetus developing properly"? The answer to the first question is a matter of good general medical supervision, and the answer to the second has been very greatly simplified by the availability of ultrasonic scanning. There are now also a number of biochemical tests available which purport to assess the functioning of the fetus and placenta by examination of the mother's blood or urine. Unfortunately, the reliability and exact relevance of these tests is still under debate. Too much reliance upon them will sometimes mean that one induces a labour unnecessarily early, with consequent risk to the baby, while ignoring a highly abnormal result may be followed by a death *in utero* which could perhaps have been avoided. Until science has advanced a little further, and the true relevance and reliability of such tests has been established, decisions will perforce be based upon clinical experience of their use, and no single clinician can acquire enough personal experience to be reliable. A system is urgently needed whereby individual experiences can be pooled and so determine the importance which should be given to each of the multitude of parameters now available. I shall urge later that randomized prospective clinical trials are needed if we are to act logically and correctly.

A further important factor which has changed obstetric practice is our increased pharmacological control over labour. It is now possible to induce and sustain premature labour when it is believed that this presents less danger to the fetus than remaining *in utero*. In the past, premature labour was induced only when pre-eclamptic toxaemia or some other easily diagnosed condition threatened the life of the fetus. Now many new tests are available which may indicate failing feto-placental function, and we also have the ability to record continuously the fetal heart rate and follow it through the ordinary uterine contractions of late pregnancy, thereby sometimes detecting irregularities suggestive of failure of the placenta. In summary, we now have tests which may suggest the need to induce premature labour and we have a vastly increased ability to do so. What we lack is objective evaluation of our new tests. This dilemma lies behind the popular controversy over the increasing use of induction of labour.

Like most obstetricians I used to teach that birth is dangerous to the fetus. I would say that the risk of perinatal death is equivalent to the total risk of death over the next twenty years. In fact I used to say that the day of one's birth is likely to be the most dangerous of one's life and I gave up the phrase only when a student remarked that the day of one's death must run it a close second. These ideas seemed to have a logical basis because the forceful uterine contractions of labour inevitably constrict the placental attachment and restrict blood-flow through it. Normally these temporary episodes of asphyxia are well within the tolerance of the fetus but many factors may exacerbate the strain and if labour has been deliberately induced early because the placental function is believed to be faulty, the risks of serious asphyxia in labour are increased. Similarly the risks in spontaneous premature and in twin labour are greater than normal. Even in the most normal of labours asphyxia may suddenly occur as, for example, when the umbilical cord happens to be coiled around the fetal neck and, with the descent of the head, is suddenly pulled tight and partially or totally obstructed.

When we look closely at data already available to us we discover that actually labour itself is not nearly as dangerous as we had thought. Only 13% of all perinatal deaths occur during labour (McIlwaine *et al.*, 1979) and most of these fetuses were already at special risk before labour had started. In most cases this was either from congenital abnormality or because the intrauterine development was unsatisfactory or had been terminated too soon and they had been born immature. If we remove all these factors, we are left with deaths due to trauma or where no underlying cause is found. Most of the latter group will be cases of true asphyxia occurring in labour, but in time to come we may discover that some proportion were due to prenatal factors. These two groups comprise those babies lost due to factors operating during labour. It would be an exaggeration to say that they represent avoidable deaths in labour but they form the closest available approximation to this.

If we accept the recent Scottish data (McIlwaine *et al.*, 1979) quoted in the Short Report (House of Commons, 1980) these two groups combined account for only 5% of all perinatal deaths. When we come to weigh the claims of new techniques designed to reduce the risks of death in labour we must bear in mind the very low proportion of deaths which are at present attributable to labour itself. Real progress in reducing perinatal deaths must come from our better understanding and avoidance of adverse factors in pregnancy.

The paramount importance of the prenatal causes of fetal loss was well recognized by the members of the Short Committee who say "On studying the evidence on current research given by the Department of Health and Social Security and the Medical Research Council, we were struck by the apparent paucity of research focused upon explaining the manifestly important role of social and dietary factors, and their effects upon the underlying causes we have discussed, and our persisting ignorance about the precipitating factors of such important conditions as multiple birth, maternal toxaemia, bleeding and preterm delivery, let alone congenital malformations" (House of Commons, 1980).

Because of our ignorance of intrauterine factors, the main concentration of technical expertise has been devoted to the management of labour itself. Currently the most important controversy in obstetrics is about the value of fetal monitoring whereby the fetal heart can be continuously recorded throughout labour. Variations in the heart rate, particularly certain patterns in the rate change, are believed to be diagnostic of asphyxia. Thus monitors can give early warning of distress in the fetus and enable appropriate action to be taken quickly. These machines were developed in the early 1960s and have been in widespread use for over a decade. They now form a routine part of the management of high-risk labour and are also used for more accurate assessment whenever clinical signs suggest that asphyxia may be developing. The use of these machines requires that the mother be virtually immobilised in labour and that obstetricians and midwives learn new skills in the interpretation of the graphs they produce. Old clinical skills and judgments are neglected only at peril to the patients, for machines can break down and by Murphy's law they will do so under the most difficult circumstances. Let us also remember that high-powered technology can cause apprehension and fear, factors which themselves may adversely affect the outcome.

The fetal monitor is basically an improved and refined way of listening to the fetal heart, something obstetricians have been doing for more than a century; it cannot tell for certain whether or not the fetus is suffering from asphyxia. More recently a technique has been developed whereby a drop of blood is taken from the fetal scalp when distress is suspected and is analysed for its acidity as an indicator of asphyxia. This test can be performed rapidly and accurately, given the necessary expensive equipment, and it is considered to be a more reliable guide to fetal status than electronic fetal monitoring. Nowadays well-equipped obstetric departments possess both facilities.

Electronic fetal heart monitoring and biochemical testing of fetal blood are theoretical advances upon clinical judgement. Their widespread use is already costing extremely large sums of money and a vast amount of clinical effort whilst there is, as yet, no conclusive evidence that they are beneficial in the management of normal low-risk labour. In the literature to date there are only four reports of clinical trials where the outcome of labour managed using these aids was compared with the outcome using clinical assessment only (Haverkamp et al., 1976; 1979; Renou et al., 1976; Kelso et al., 1978; Chalmers, 1979). These trials were all relatively small numerically and in total only 2,030 women took part. In none was the superiority of the new technology established and the only significant finding, common to all four trials, was that the caesarean section rate was doubled for women monitored, without demonstrable improvement in fetal outcome. One finding was that out of a total of 13 new-born infants suffering fits, only four came from mothers who had been monitored: this difference does suggest that fetal monitoring is of value for fetuses at severe risk. What is obvious is that these four trials, the only objective evidence yet available, are inadequate for a proper assessment of this very important problem. We need much larger trials, preferably undertaken simultaneously in several different centres, if we are to make an objective assessment of the new obstetrics.

The second big issue in perinatal care is the value of intensive care of new-born babies — an issue even more clouded with emotional overtones and therefore even more difficult to assess rationally. As far as monitoring in labour is concerned, the supporters maintain that it provides more reliable safeguards against transient asphyxia in labour and so may be protecting some fetuses, even though it cannot yet be shown to save lives. The importance of perinatal asphyxia as a possible causative factor in later childhood disability is the crux of the problem.

In studying this possible correlation, great care must be exercised to avoid confusion with other perinatal factors such as immaturity or dysmaturity (small-for-dates babies), because these are often grouped together and, by implication, the final outcome is incorrectly ascribed to avoidable factors in perinatal care. It would seem that the very high estimates of salvable babies quoted in the Short Report must be due to this confusion.

Cerebral palsy is one of the few handicapping conditions in childhood which can be definitely linked with abnormal perinatal events. It is not a single entity but in all its various forms it causes disorders of movement and posture due to a non-progressive defect or lesion of the brain in early life. The basic causes include disorders of cerebral development and cell migration, intrauterine infections, perinatal asphyxia and many post-natal causes such as kernicterus (gross jaundice usually due to rhesus disease), meningitis or trauma. Of all these causes of cerebral palsy only asphyxia during and immediately after birth, trauma and kernicterus are factors where skilled management by obstetrician or paediatrician could influence the outcome. Examination of the child with cerebral palsy can only rarely indicate whether the condition followed perinatal events or had a different cause.

The same problem exists with other forms of handicap. Drillien (1978) has written: "In the absence of other clues one is faced with the 'chicken and egg' dilemma; is the child profoundly retarded because of hypoxic brain damage at birth which could have been avoided if resuscitative facilities had been available, or did the infant both fail to breathe and present as neurologically abnormal because of pre-existing brain malformation?''

Numerous longitudinal studies have shown that socio-economic factors have a far greater effect upon outcome than do perinatal events (Sameroff and Chandler, 1975). We assess the new-born baby for what we unscientifically describe as the effect of asphyxia (there may actually be pre-natal causes), by the Apgar test and in a very large American study children with a low Apgar score (Drage et al., 1964) at birth had slightly lower intelligent quotients on the Stanford-Binet tests at the age of four than those with high Apgar scores. The difference between the two groups was four I.Q. points. On the other hand, within each group of infants defined by Apgar score, there was an 18 point I.Q. difference between social groups indexed by the mother's level of education. From the point of view of the fetus the choice of parents is far more important than the choice of obstetrician.

There is evidence that the brain of the immature fetus, the one exposed to premature delivery, spontaneous or induced, can withstand oxygen deprivation better than that of the mature or post-mature fetus. Also there is evidence that short periods of oxygen-lack, such as may occur in labour, even when severe, are less damaging than prolonged, though presumably less severe, oxygen-lack *in utero*. This forms the basis upon which induction of labour for placental insufficiency is based.

The primary justification for intensive care units for the new-born is in the care of premature and light-for-dates babies. Technical advances in this field have been comparable with the introduction of fetal monitoring. There is no doubt that with intensive care more babies of low (less than 2,500 grams) and very low (less than 1,500 grams) birth-weights now survive. The question not yet answered is how many of the survivors will suffer severe handicap. A report from the Hammersmith Hospital (McIlwaine *et al.*, 1979) surveyed 357 babies born there between 1961 and 1975 with birth-weights of 501 to 1,500 grams. At follow-up 27.8 per cent of these babies were apparently normal, 5.6 per cent had developed minor handicap and 5.3 per cent major handicap: the others had died, nearly all shortly after birth. The authors state that there was no significant improvement in the proportion of handicapped children among these very low-weight liveborn children throughout the 15-year period, despite increasing complexity of care. They comment that the long-term safety of some of the present effective forms of treatment has yet to be established and they suggest that further study of outcome in defined communities would be wise.

There have been numerous other reports, in particular from Sweden, of follow-up studies of babies treated in intensive care units and the data are conflicting. It is clear that comparing different hospitals or communities is fraught with potential error. Ideally a prospective trial where infants at risk were randomly allocated to a group having intensive care or to a group receiving ordinary good clinical care under the same paediatricians is the optimal way in which we should be able to assess the value and/or dangers of the new techniques. There is only one such randomized prospective trial which was carried out at the Royal Women's Hospital, Melbourne, between 1966 and 1970 (Kitchen *et al.*, 1979). The findings suggested that the increased survival of new-born infants receiving intensive care was achieved at the expense of producing additional severely handicapped children. This trial involved techniques now outdated but it was successful in saving new-born lives and our current therapy may one day be shown to be equally liable to cause handicap. Intensive care of the new-born does save lives and for this reason there are obvious ethical difficulties in setting up further clinical trials, but unless they are established we shall never be sure that we are not causing increased handicap by one or other facet of our new techniques.

The present position is summarized in the recent paper on cerebral palsy which surveys the literature (Macfarlane, 1980) and the author concludes: "Estimates seem to give a figure of approximately 5–6 per cent for the total incidence of moderate or severe physical handicap and intellectual retardation per year in children. With approximately 600,000 births this represents 35,000 handicapped children of which 1,000 might be handicapped by perinatal events; that is 2.6 per cent of the total handicapped paediatric population". It is obvious that the importance of delivery and immediate post-delivery events such as transient anoxia have been greatly over-estimated in the past and that, as with perinatal mortality, the really important period, and the one about which we have least hard information, is intrauterine development.

Once sufficient data have been collected about any condition or disease its treatment rapidly becomes standardized. The treatment of diseases of the thyroid or prostatic enlargement or of common fractures vary only marginally between different practitioners. In obstetrics this is not so. An English woman is nearly three times as likely to have her labour induced as a Norwegian. Within this country recently reported induction rates vary from 15 per cent to 55 per cent of all deliveries (Chalmers and Richards, 1977). Similarly in 1972 the Leeds Region had a forceps delivery rate of 7.1 whereas in Oxford the rate was 13.4. In the same year caesarean section rates varied from 2.9 for East Anglia to 6.0 for Liverpool. Those who object to randomized clinical trials because some patients may thereby be deprived of optimal treatment might reflect that in practice the randomized variation in treatment which a woman may expect according to her area of residence is likely to be at least as great.

Obstetricians fall into two groups: interventionists who monitor many parameters of fetal well-being and growth and who interfere when these values vary from the accepted norm and conservatives who tend to intervene as little as possible on the grounds that the dangers of such intervention may well exceed the risks.

Such a classification is an over-simplification but the variations in clinical practice prove that we lack the ability to assess the importance of our new parameters of fetal distress and thereby to weigh them logically against the dangers of obstetric intervention.

Even when reliable information is made available we do not always recognize its validity. In 1922 a randomized prospective trial showed that shaving the genital area as part of the preparation for labour did not reduce the incidence of infection (Johnson and Sidall, 1922). In 1965 a further prospective trial confirmed this finding (Kantor *et al.*, 1965); but even today many women are submitted to this uncomfortable and unnecessary procedure.

All medical innovations involve risk. If we want progress we must accept that every new drug and every new procedure may disclose iatrogenic risk which becomes manifest only after clinical use. Before any new drug is made generally available there are extensive animal trials and a prospective clinical trial is virtually mandatory. What is peculiar is that we have made little attempt to exercise the same caution and scientific testing of innovatory clinical procedures. Thousands of babies were blinded by excessive and prolonged oxygen administration during resuscitation but there has been no public reaction as there was following the thalidomide disaster. The reason is that no one doubts the sincerity of the paediatricians who administered the oxygen. What is certain is that if the resuscitation procedure had been adequately monitored from the time when high concentrations of oxygen were first used for significant periods of time, the effect would have been recognized more quickly and many babies would have been saved from blindness.

The ethics of the randomized prospective clinical trial have been a subject of much confused thinking. Once a drug or technique has been proven to be of value it is clearly unethical to withhold it from a random group of patients for research purposes. To extend this ethical argument to the point where it is held to be wrong to withhold what is merely believed to be beneficial because of possible deprivation, is to pass judgement in advance of trial. There is a good example of such confusion. A New York paediatrician, at the time when a very high protein diet was being postulated as beneficial in pregnancy, proposed a randomized trial of protein supplements (Rush *et al.*, 1980). His hospital ethical committee at first refused permission on the grounds that the supplements should be offered to all. Fortunately the trial was finally approved and showed that the control group did better than those receiving the supplements. Very high protein diets are not now recommended.

Perinatal deaths are falling. With modern intensive care more babies of very low birth-weight are surviving. The number of handicapped children appears constant. There is no obvious relationship between the fall in perinatal mortality and the incidence of handicap.

When we seek the causes of perinatal death and of handicap in children, it appears that truly perinatal causes, that is, events occurring at or near birth, account for only a very small proportion of either. We urgently need research into origins of defective development in pregnancy which is the main cause of perinatal death and of handicap.

Obstetricians have enthusiastically accepted the tools of modern scientific research but have failed to apply scientific discipline to their assessment in clinical practice. If the quality of care is to improve this discipline will have to be implemented.

When I undertook this lecture I thought that I should be able to present a review of the New Obstetrics and show how our very definite improvements in reproductive statistics have been achieved. In particular I believed that our increased use of fetal monitoring was an important advance in obstetrics. At that stage I would have said, as the Short Report in summary does say, that with more doctors and better equipment we could eliminate many avoidable deaths and cases of handicap. Having reviewed the medical literature I cannot honestly say any of these things. This does not mean all such optimistic assumptions are false, only that reasonable proof of their truth is lacking.

I have come to the conclusion that we still need to consider very carefully how we can best improve our maternity services and that the most important part of the reproductive process, and the one about which we know the least, is intrauterine development. Research into this field is urgent and we could usefully start by investigating why it is that social class makes such a vast difference.

References

Alberman, E. (1977). Facts and figures. In *Benefits and Hazards of the New Obstetrics*. Edited by T. Chard and M. P. M. Richards. Clinics in Developmental Medicine, No. 64. London: Spastics International Medical Publications/Heinemann Medical Books.

Anderson, A. B. M. (1979). Prevention of preterm labour. In *Human Parturition: New Concepts and Developments*. Edited by M. J. M. C. Keirse, pp. 235–245. The Hague: Leiden University Press.

Chalmers, I. (1979). Randomized controlled trial of intrapartum fetal monitoring 1973–1977. In *Perinatal Medicine*. Edited by O. Thalhammer, K. Baumgarten and A. Pollak, pp. 260–265. Stuttgart: Georg Thieme.

Chalmers, I. and Richards, M. P. M. (1977). Intervention and causal inference in obstetric practice. In *Benefits and Hazards of the New Obstetrics*. Edited by T. Chard and M. P. M. Richards, pp. 34–61. Clinics in Developmental Medicine, No. 64. London: Spastics International Medical Publications/Heinemann Medical Books.

Chamberlain, R., Chamberlain, G., Howlett, B. and Claireaux, A. (1975). *British Births 1970*. Vol. 1. *The First Week of Life*. London: Heinemann Medical Books.

Davies, I. M. (1980). Perinatal and infant deaths: social and biological factors. *Population Trends*, **19**, 19–21. London: HMSO.

Drage, J. S., Kennedy, C. and Schwarz, B. K. (1964). The Apgar score as an index of infant morbidity: a report from the collaborative study on cerebral palsy. *Obstetrics and Gynecology*, **24**, 222–230.

Drillien, C. M. (1978). Aetiology of severely handicapping conditions in early childhood. In *Major Mental Handicap: Methods and Costs of Prevention*. Edited by K. Elliot and M. O'Connor, p. 19. CIBA Foundation Symposium 59 (new series). Amsterdam: Elsevier.

Haverkamp, A. D., Thompson, H. E., McFee, J. G. and Cetrulo, C. (1976). The evaluation of continuous fetal heart rate monitoring in high-risk pregnancy. *American Journal of Obstetrics and Gynecology*, **125**, 310–320.

Haverkamp, A. D., Orleans, M., Langendoerfer, S., McFee, J. G., Murphy, J. and Thompson, H. E. (1979). A controlled trial of the differential effects of intrapartum fetal monitoring. *American Journal of Obstetrics and Gynecology*, **134**, 399–412.

Home Office (1978). *Criminal Statistics*. Cmnd. 7670. London: HMSO.

House of Commons (1980). *Perinatal and Neonatal Mortality*. Second Report from the Social Services Committee, Session 1979–80. Vol. I. *Report*. Cmnd. 663–1. London: HMSO.

Huntingford, P. (1978). Obstetric practice: past, present and the future. In *The Place of Birth: A Study of the Environment in which Birth Takes Place with Special Reference to Home Confinement*. Edited by S. Kitzinger and J. A. Davis. Oxford: Oxford University Press.

Illingworth, R. S. (1979). Why blame the obstetrician? A review. *British Medical Journal*, **i**, 797–801.

Johnston, R. and Sidall, R. S. (1922). Is the usual method of preparing patients for delivery beneficial or necessary? *American Journal of Obstetrics and Gynecology*, **4**, 645–650.

Jones, R. A. K., Cummins, M. and Davies, P. A. (1979). Infants of very low birthweight: a fifteen-year analysis. *Lancet*, **i**, 1332–1335.

Kantor, H. I., Rember, R., Tabio, P. and Buchanon, R. (1965). Value of shaving the pudendal-perineal area in delivery preparation. *Obstetrics and Gynecology*, **25**, 509–512.

Kelso, I. M., Parsons, R. J., Lawrence, F. G., Arora, S. S., Edmonds, D. K. and Cooke, I. D. (1978). An assessment of continuous fetal heart rate monitoring in labour: a randomized trial. *American Journal of Obstetrics and Gynecology*, **131**, 526–532.

Kitchen, W. H., Richards, A., Ryann, M. M., McDougall, A. B., Billson, E. A., Kier, E. H. and Naylor, F. D. (1979). A longitudinal study of very low birthweight infants. II. Results of a controlled trial of intensive care and incidence of handicap. *Developmental Medicine and Child Neurology*, **21**, 582–589.

Macfarlane, A. (1979). Social class variations in perinatal mortality. *Journal of Maternal and Child Health*, **4**, 337–340.

Macfarlane, J. A. (1980). Studies of cerebral palsy. In *Perinatal Audit and Survaillance*. Edited by I. Chalmers and G. McIlwaine. London: Royal College of Obstetricians and Gynaecologists.

McIlwaine, G. M., Howat, R. C. L., Dunn, F. and Macnaughton, M. C. (1979). The Scottish perinatal mortality survey. *British Medical Journal*, **ii**, 1103–1106.

Renou, P., Chang, A., Anderson, I. and Wood, C. (1976). Controlled trial of fetal intensive care. *American Journal of Obstetrics and Gynecology*, **126**, 470–476.

Rush, D., Stein, Z. and Susser M. (1980). A randomized controlled trial of pre-natal nutritional supplementation in New York City. *Pediatrics*, **65**, 683–697.

Sameroff, A. J. and Chandler, M. J. (1975). Reproductive risk and the continuum of care-taking causality. In *Review of Child Development Research*. Edited by F. D. Horowitz, M. Hetherington, S. Scarr-Salapatek and G. Siegal, Vol. 4, Pt. 4, pp. 187–244. Chicago: University of Chicago Press.

Evaluation of Perinatal Practice:
The Limitations of Audit by Death

IAIN CHALMERS

National Perinatal Epidemiology Unit,
Radcliffe Infirmary, Oxford

In the minds of many, those working in the field of perinatal medicine have seemed to exemplify how clinical practitioners should go about evaluating the quality of their work. Yet, as one obstetrician has recently remarked, in spite of the fact that few countries can equal the self-critical analysis to which obstetricians in Britain regularly submit themselves, British obstetrics and neonatal paediatrics seem to be going through a bad patch during which the best of intentions seem to have turned sour (Barron, 1979).

Perinatal practice has been the subject of intense and more or less continuous public debate for the last seven years. The debate gathered momentum following a report by the Oxford Consumer Group early in 1974: a survey of public opinions of the health services uncovered more adverse comments about the maternity service than about any other branch of the National Health Service (Robinson, 1974). It is particularly interesting that the report related to a city with a brand new maternity hospital, relatively favourable staffing levels, and one of the lowest perinatal mortality rates in the United Kingdom (Chalmers, 1976).

This example raises questions concerning the criteria and methods which have been used to evaluate perinatal practice. These activities, which we may term perinatal audit, have always been dominated by the attention given to death. In former times, it was particularly maternal deaths which prompted enquiries concerned to identify deficiencies in the quality of care. The enormous variability in maternal mortality rates and the actual modes of maternal death strongly suggest that estimates of the crude risk of maternal death do indeed reflect the quality of perinatal care. However, quite apart from the need to assess the impact of other factors influencing the estimated risk (Newcombe *et al.*, 1975), and the lack of any hard evidence that formal audit of maternal deaths has reduced their incidence (Grimes, 1977), the extreme infrequency of maternal deaths limits their usefulness for perinatal audit.

More recently, perinatal audit has focused on baby deaths. In some respects this emphasis on death in perinatal audit is understandable. Deaths are more easily defined and enumerated than other parameters which might be used to audit practice. But even so, there are worrying variations in the manner in which the fundamental step of enumeration is made. Validation studies have shown how neonatal deaths can be under-registered by as much as 20 per cent, even in countries with relatively sophisticated vital statistics systems (McCarthy *et al.*, 1980; Scott *et al.*, 1981). There continue to be discrepancies (first noted in 1910 (Stevenson, 1910)) between the numbers of vital events recorded, on the one hand, through the system of midwives' notifications to local health authorities and, on the other hand, registrations recorded by Registrars of Births, Marriages and Deaths. The following example illustrates the errors that can occur unless careful quality control is maintained in collecting these basic vital statistics:

An Area Medical Officer received (as is routine procedure) a copy of a still-birth *registration* from the local Registrar. This indicated that a still-birth certificate had been given to the parent by the appropriate person in the hospital where the still-birth had occurred.

However, no matching birth *notification* form had been received from the obstetric unit. When contacted by telephone, the ward sister first claimed no knowledge of any still-birth, saying that the patient was in the private care of a consultant obstetrician and that he should be asked for further information. It was pointed out to her that the law required notification and registration of every birth, whether live or still, whether privately assisted or otherwise. Alternatively, if there had been no still-birth, a declaration to the Registrar cancelling the still-birth registration was required.

A birth notification was finally forthcoming.

Both still-births and live-births (Richards, 1980) can be "lost" as abortions in this way and substantial variations in the estimated risk of perinatal death can result from these variations in recording (Scott *et al.*, 1981). As one step towards increasing comparability between statistics, it seems wise to adopt the recommendation contained in the ninth revision of the International Classification of Diseases (World Health Organization, 1978): national perinatal statistics should include all fetuses and infants delivered weighing at least 500g., whether alive or dead. To conform with these recommendations, *all* babies should be weighed at, or soon after birth. There are good clinical reasons for weighing even the illest babies (Wilkinson and Howat, 1980; Scanlon, 1980), and this basic information should be available for every baby without exception. However, even if the enumeration of perinatal deaths can be standardized and improved, questions remain about their use for perinatal audit. Although perinatal deaths are more numerous than maternal deaths, variation in their frequency correlates poorly with variation in indices of perinatal care (Bakketeig *et al.*, 1978; Macfarlane *et al.*, 1980). Perinatal mortality reflects pathological processes which are much less clearly understood than the infections and haemorrhages which have killed so many mothers.

Explicit acknowledgement of this ignorance has been encouraged by those who have stressed the necessity of categorizing a considerable proportion of perinatal deaths as "cause not known" (Baird *et al.*, 1954). More commonly, however, jargon is used to obscure our ignorance. There are dangers inherent in this practice. Firstly it may hinder the careful search required to elucidate pathological mechanisms; secondly it may encourage unduly simplistic inferences about methods of clinical practice; thirdly it may promote unrealistic expectations among clinicians and parents alike concerning the preventability of perinatal deaths (Mitchell and Chalmers, 1980). Thus, if deaths for which no obvious cause can be found are labelled as having resulted from "anoxia" or "asphyxia", an assumption is encouraged that they are preventable by intervening to make oxygen available — for example, by expediting delivery of a fetus showing signs of "distress", or artificially ventilating the lungs of an apnoeic infant. Even without formally testing such assumptions in clinical experiments, it is certain that a proportion of such deaths is indeed preventable by using such methods (Spellacy *et al.*, 1975; Neldam, 1980). Just what proportion may be preventable is less clear. Carefully conducted post-mortem examinations may help to clarify whether these "anoxic deaths" are associated with, for example, cardiac malformations, myocardial necrosis associated with coronary arterial lesions (de Sa, 1979), or other conditions which may remain undetected without careful necropsies. Such undetected abnormalities may render babies less responsive to the clinical interventions which have been proposed to prevent so-called "anoxic/asphyxic" deaths. But, quite apart from the problem of undetected, but detectable, abnormalities, it will probably always be difficult to assess the extent to which "fetal distress" and "neonatal apnoea/asphyxia" may be *late* expressions of fundamental abnormalities which are even less easily recognized (Drillien, 1978). Considering the substantial and still poorly understood loss of fetuses in early pregnancy (Fox, 1978; Miller *et al.*, 1980) it would seem prudent not to assume that all deaths in later pregnancy in which clinical and post-mortem signs of asphyxia are the sole findings are necessarily caused simply by "lack of oxygen". These problems have not prevented the widespread use of crude analyses of perinatal mortality statistics by those who have sought a simple way of characterizing the quality of perinatal care. This abuse of statistics has been discussed elsewhere (Chalmers *et al.*, 1980). The risk of perinatal death in a particular population is largely determined by the proportion of low-weight births and the frequency of lethal or serious congenital malformations (Chalmers and Macfarlane, 1980). Any attempt to derive statistics which reflect the quality of perinatal care must take these factors into account (Macfarlane *et al.*, 1980; Wigglesworth, 1980). Estimates of the risk of death from causes other than malformations at a given birth-weight seem likely to reflect the quality of perinatal care rather better (Bakketeig *et al.*, 1978). But even so, there are assumptions involved in the use of birth-weight-specific mortality rates among normally-formed babies (similar to those relating to the "cause labels" referred to above) which require further evaluation (Macfarlane *et al.*, 1980; Russell and Wilcox, 1980).

It is in the light of these uncertainties that no less an authority than Sir Dugald Baird has warned of the dangers inherent in the concept of "avoidable perinatal deaths" (Baird, 1980). Yet claims concerning the "avoidability" of death (and, more recently, "handicap") have pervaded both the training of clinicians and public discussions of perinatal health services; the single most publicized opinion of the Select Committee on *Perinatal and Neonatal Mortality* was its view that the universal application of modern knowledge and care could lead to the prevention, every year, of between 3000 and 5000 still-births and neonatal deaths, and of important handicaps in a further 5000 children (House of Commons, 1980).

At best, claims such as these might be interpreted as wishful thinking by those who are unwilling to be constrained by the lack of supporting evidence; at worst, they could be interpreted as an opportunistic attempt to secure yet more resources for further intensifying and centralizing perinatal care in full knowledge of the fact that there is little hard evidence to justify such policies. While it is clear that developments in the support of small babies have increased their survival chances (Roberton, 1977; Kitchen *et al.*, 1979), it is less clear what the impact of the more intensive approaches to perinatal care has been on the *overall* chances of a baby surviving with a severe handicap. As Macfarlane has observed in an important review of the available information (Macfarlane, 1980), "reducing the risk of perinatal death is by no means always accompanied by a reduction in morbidity of perinatal origin".

If only for this reason, the obsession with death is inappropriate. Information on death must be assessed in conjunction with information on the status of survivors, both during the neonatal period and in later childhood (Hey, 1980). In general, neonatal indices are poor predictors of subsequent handicap (Sameroff and Chandler, 1975); but convulsions during the first two or three days of life are an exception and may prove to be a satisfactory neonatal marker of poor perinatal care (Dennis, 1978). Later progress should be assessed by monitoring the increased morbidity and hospital readmission rates experienced by graduates of intensive perinatal care (Hack *et al.*, 1981) and by paying particular attention to changes in the birth cohort prevalence of cerebral palsy, blindness and deafness.

But there are other, quite separate reasons for challenging the dominance of death in perinatal audit. To illustrate the problem one might observe that about 800 perinatal deaths could be "prevented" in England and Wales every year by the simple measure of routine ultrasound examinations during the first trimester of pregnancy. In this way multiple pregnancies, which are at high risk of poor perinatal outcome, could be identified and terminated. The fact that this suggestion is insensitive is irrelevant, for so also are several measures which have already been espoused and implemented in the frenetic race to lower perinatal mortality rates at all costs. Because clinicians have been conditioned during years of training and experience to remember the catastrophic departures from normality which can supervene during the course of pregnancy, child-birth and early infancy, it is all too easy for them to forget that the vast majority of women can bear children satisfactorily without specialist medical attention. Perhaps it is this distorted perspective which has led to the patterns of perinatal care about which there is so much dissatisfaction, for any audit of perinatal practice which is restricted to a consideration of the one woman in fifty who loses a baby is clearly going to be seriously deficient.

The lengths to which perinatal specialists are prepared to go in their poorly evaluated and costly efforts to increase perinatal survival rates above the 98–99 per cent which is now characteristic of populations in most developed countries are eloquently illustrated by the explosive growth in the use of caesarean section (Fig. 1).

So alarming are these trends in the United States that both the Department of Health, Education and Welfare (Marieskind, 1979) and the National Institutes of Health (Perry and Kalberer, 1980) have

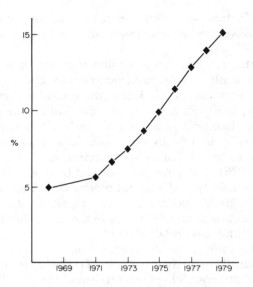

FIG. 1. Caesarean sections as a proportion of all deliveries, United States, 1968–1979. (Marieskind, 1979).

initiated studies to analyse the phenomenon. Variations in the use of caesarean section may, to some extent, reflect the different "needs" of the population served. Thus in populations in which true cephalo-pelvic disproportion is a relatively common obstetric problem, a relatively high caesarean section rate would be expected. However, variation in clinical practice is so great that it is reasonable to assume that other factors play an important role in determining variation in the use of this and other medical interventions (Chalmers and Richards, 1977). The list of likely influences is long, but there is evidence that clinical intervention is affected by culture, tradition, status and fashion; by the availability of buildings, personnel, hospital beds and equipment; by the need to provide opportunities for clinicians in training to gain experience; by fear of malpractice litigation; by the extent to which doctors are paid on a "piecework" basis, and by commercial pressures from drug and equipment manufacturers and others (Fig. 2).

In Britain, we are fortunate that clinicians are not yet subject to all these influences. Ideally, clinical judgments concerning treatment should be based on the practitioner's clinical assessment of the individual needs of each woman and her baby (including her own expressed preferences), tempered by reference to scientific evidence

FIG. 2. Determinants of medical intervention.

supporting the course of action which he or she proposes. Any influences which intrude upon this process are likely to operate against the best interests of mothers and babies.

Unfortunately, the scientific evidence which is so essential to this process is often not available. Thus some of the variation in caesarean section rates is due to differing opinions about the place of the operation — for example, in delivering immature fetuses or those presenting by the breech, or when the uterus is scarred as the result of a previous caesarean section. Such differences of opinion should be addressed by seeking guidance from the results of appropriately designed randomized controlled trials because the price of such uncertainty can be considerable. For example, if the United States' caesarean section rate in 1976 had been applied to our own population, nearly 35,000 additional caesarean sections would have been performed in England and Wales in 1976 at an estimated additional cost of about £18,000,000. Furthermore, we might have expected between 15 and 30 additional maternal deaths to have been associated with this major surgical procedure and its attendant hazards.

One of the factors contributing to increased caesarean section rates (Marieskind, 1979) — continuous electronic fetal heart rate monitoring — illustrates further how patterns of perinatal care can become distorted if death is dominant in attempts to assess its quality. Evidence derived from the four randomized controlled trials of this and other more intensive methods of intrapartum monitoring is unambiguous (Haverkamp et al., 1976; Renou et al., 1976; Kelso et al., 1978; Haverkamp et al., 1979): caesarean section for both "fetal distress" (Table I) and the "catch-all" diagnosis (Marieskind, 1979) of "failure to progress in labour" (Table II) is considerably more frequently performed in association with the intensive methods of fetal monitoring.

Table I
Distribution of 78 caesarean sections indicated by fetal distress among 2027 women participating in RCTs of intensive intrapartum fetal monitoring (1973–1977), by study centre and study group (Chalmers, 1979)

	Intermittent auscultation	Continuous electronic monitoring	Continuous electronic monitoring + biochemical assessment
Denver (1973–1975)	3	18	—
Melbourne (1974–1975)	9	—	16
Denver (1975–1977)	1	16	8
Sheffield (1976–1977)	3	4	—

Table II
Distribution of 91 caesarean sections for "failure to progress in labour" among 1544 women participating in the three RCTs of intensive intrapartum fetal monitoring (1974–1977), by study centre and study group (Chalmers, 1979)

	Intermittent auscultation	Continuous electronic monitoring	Continuous electronic monitoring + biochemical assessment
Melbourne (1974–1975)	7	—	10
Denver (1976–1977)	12	21	18
Sheffield (1976–1977)	7	16	—

The search for evidence of beneficial effects to compensate for this increased surgical intervention has yielded little in the way of firm conclusions (Banta and Thacker, 1979a), although there is some evidence that continuous electronic monitoring of the fetal heart rate, combined with assessment of fetal acid-base status by scalp blood sampling, may be protective against neonatal convulsions among babies at high risk of perinatal complications (Table III). These uncertainties were reflected in an authoritative report produced by a United States National Institute of Child Health and Human Development Task Force on "Predictors of fetal distress". It concluded that "periodic auscultation of the fetal heart . . . is an acceptable method of assessing fetal condition for women of low risk intrapartum fetal distress" (National Institutes of Health, 1979). The

Table III

Distribution of 13 cases of convulsions among 2032 subjects participating in RCTs of intensive intrapartum fetal monitoring (1973–1977), by study centre and study group (Chalmers, 1979)

	Intermittent auscultation	Continuous electronic monitoring	Continuous electronic monitoring + biochemical assessment
Denver (1973–1975)	2	2	—
Melbourne (1974–1975)	4	—	0
Denver (1975–1977)	2	2	0
Sheffield (1976–1977)	1	0	—

Task Force further indicated that randomized controlled trials were required to assess the place of continuous fetal heart-rate monitoring in various categories of high-risk cases.

By contrast, the British Select Committee on Perinatal and Neonatal Mortality recommended that "continuous recording of the fetal heart-rate should increasingly become part of the surveillance of all babies during labour" (House of Commons, 1980). Even if only 70 per cent of the fetuses born in England were monitored in this way, the direct costs to the tax payer would be considerable. The annual bill for scalp electrodes and recording paper alone would be nearly £2,000,000. One of the reasons for this recommendation must have been the Committee's espousal of the concept of "absolute safety" (House of

Commons, 1980, paragraph 221) for, on the evidence received and published in their report, members must have known that intrapartum deaths with either no clear cause or from trauma constituted only 7 per cent of all perinatal deaths (McIlwaine *et al.*, 1979). More worryingly, other interests may have been operating: the name of the principal British manufacturer of fetal monitors was actually spelled out for the benefit of those who attended the press conference at which the Committee's report was launched. Perinatal intensive care is big business and past experience has demonstrated how important it is to assess the nature of the vested interests of those who promote it (Banta and Thacker, 1979b).

Because of the intrusion of "needs" other than those of child-bearing women into perinatal decision-making, clinical practices need constant monitoring and evaluation. Sometimes this may be achieved through promoting better communication between professionals by using problem-oriented medical records, holding "death-and-complications" and "unit review" meetings, or providing a clinical information service (McColl *et al.*, 1976; Womersley and MacDonald, 1980). Audit of this nature [for example, to assess hysterectomy use (Dyck *et al.*, 1977), or cardiac pacemaker insertion (Friedman *et al.*, 1980)], has shown how it is possible to stem epidemics of medical intervention such as those which are currently afflicting perinatal medicine.

Such audit should be conducted in the context of relevant experimentally-derived evidence. Many writers have put forward cogent arguments for insisting on this emphasis (Chalmers, 1974; Kerr, 1975; Silverman, 1980). As Diggory observes elsewhere in this volume: "At present we are bemused by our technology and confused by our ethical uncertainties to such an extent that we have largely abandoned scientific methodology . . . . Obstetricians have enthusiastically accepted the tools of modern scientific research but have failed to apply scientific discipline to their assessment of clinical practice" (Diggory, 1981).

The extent to which this indiscipline has been a feature of perinatal practice has recently been reviewed by Silverman (Silverman, 1980). His monograph (appropriately subtitled *A Modern Parable*) should be required reading for all those wishing to practise perinatal medicine. He draws our attention to the way in which obstetricians and paediatricians, with their past record of having embraced fashionable, but in retrospect, disastrous modes of intervention, continue to be unwilling to assess the affects of their actions by using the "risk-minimizing" strategy of the randomized controlled trial.

The most encouraging single example of the existence of a professional will to correct this state of affairs is the initiative launched by the Canadian Medical Research Council's Workshop on Perinatology (Medical Research Council of Canada, 1979). If the Canadian Committee for the Promotion of Clinical Trials in Perinatal Medicine can successfully foster the multicentre collaboration which is required to answer many of the questions posed by current perinatal practice, its creation will deserve to be regarded as a landmark in the development of perinatal research.

The Canadian MRC initiative also draws attention to the need to assess the effectiveness and safety *in common clinical practice* of interventions shown to be efficacious and relatively safe in the controlled conditions of an experimental evaluation. In this respect, developments in methods used to evaluate the quality of surgical practice (Luft *et al.*, 1979) may be relevant to the perinatal field. Clinical acumen in diagnosis (Lynch and Roberts, 1977; Dennis, 1978) and clinical skill in applying interventions are clearly relevant variables in any audit of practice. Yet these important qualities have received little explicit attention from either commentators or researchers (Chalmers *et al.*, 1980). The issue was summed up well by an obstetrician who gave evidence to the Select Committee on Perinatal and Neonatal Mortality (Blunt, 1979). He told the Committee that although the amount of monitoring equipment had recently been increased at his hospital, he considered the quality of the staff to be of far greater importance in determining the standard of the service provided.

Developing and maintaining the clinical skills of those practising in the perinatal field is clearly a desirable objective of perinatal audit. A minority of women and babies will always require obstetric and neonatal intervention, often in an unpredictable emergency. It is clearly preferable if such interventions are administered with the technical skill which comes from practice and experience. The issue is clearly illustrated by Doughty's not-unreasonable equivalence between the frequency with which epidural anaesthesia is used in obstetric practice and the safety and efficiency with which the intervention is conducted (Fig. 3).

But this raises *the* fundamental problem facing perinatologists and childbearing women. For, among other things, it is the increased intervention and centralization of care deriving from a "technically excellent", "absolute safety", "death orientated" approach to childbirth that has led to public dissatisfaction with the services. As Bardon has suggested, what is required is an acknowledgement by

FIG. 3. Incidence of epidural analgesia during labour and adjudged quality of service, London teaching hospitals (Doughty, 1978).

everyone involved that "the concept of absolute safety is illusory, and the health of mothers and babies is in danger when safety is equated with anything short of being dead. The development of health is something much more than not being dead. It involves the persistent taking of calculated risks gladly and responsibly. So also "does the practice of professionalism" (Bardon, 1980). In other words, clinical expertise requires not only technical skill, but the ability to decide when and how to deploy it.

The consequences of pursuing the mirage of "absolute safety" have been well illustrated by McIlwaine and her colleagues (McIlwaine *et al.*, 1979). Reviewing the results of their survey of perinatal deaths in Scotland they observed that 47 out of 1122 perinatal deaths might have been prevented by a policy of routine induction at 40 weeks gestation; but this would also have required the induction of 37,000 labours. They call for a sense of perspective in the use of intervention which includes a reckoning of the negative effects in terms of the stress and anxiety imposed on pregnant women. This view echoes Farrant's assessment of the effects of a screening programme introduced to identify and eliminate by abortion fetuses with open neural tube defects. Women referred for amniocentesis as a result of a relatively high serum alpha-fetoprotein detected during population screening were considerably more anxious than those who knew already that they were at increased risk of bearing an abnormal child (Farrant, 1980).

Table IV
Emotional reaction to the experience of waiting for the result of prenatal diagnosis, according to indication for amniocentesis (Farrant, 1980)

	Indication for amniocentesis	
	High serum alpha-fetoprotein	Other
Found the experience:	(n = 33)	(n = 57)
Not, a little, or moderately distressing	21%	86%
Very or extremely distressing	79%	14%
Could stop worrying:	(n = 33)	(n = 56)
Yes	33%	87%
No	67%	13%
Suffered from:	(n = 31)	(n = 55)
Depressed mood	71%	24%
Crying	71%	9%
Irritability	57%	20%
Poor concentration	53%	7%
Headaches	35%	16%
Sleep disturbance	61%	16%
Loss of appetite	65%	5%
> 3 of the above	71%	9%

All differences between groups are significant at the $p < 0.001$ level (X^2, 1 d.f.).

Public reactions to the strategies which the medical profession has adopted to cope with the uncertainties which are an inevitable concomitant of childbearing (Maclean, 1975) suggest that customer audit of perinatal practice is less "death-orientated" than medical audit. The following letter, sent by two community health councillors to *The Guardian*, illustrates the difference in perspective which can exist:

Factors other than health of mothers and babies would appear to determine the extent of the use of technology in obstetrics. If they did not, the variation in use might be considerably less.

For example, in City and East London Area Health Authority we have two large teaching hospitals drawing their patients from very similar catchment areas, doing roughly the same number of deliveries. The two medical schools have a joint professor of obstetrics and gynaecology. Thus the two hospitals might be expected to have similar intervention rates.

In fact there are major variations. At St. Bartholomew's Hospital 18% of babies were born by caesarean section in 1979, and 22% by forceps, while at the London Hospital only 12% were born by caesarean section and 8% by forceps.

Variations like these cannot be attributed to differences in "at risk" factors.

The effects of being born by caesarean section may have long-term psychological and emotional consequences for mothers and babies. Certainly we are very aware in this district of the long-term consequences of many episiotomies (about 90% of women at Bart's have episiotomies while less than 35% of women at the London Hospital end up with one).

The various rates and policies of obstetric units ought to be widely available so that women can discuss with their GPs what type of care is most suitable for them. An independent monitoring system should be set up into the use of technology in obstetrics. We do not think that this investigation should have to wait until variations show up in the death rate. (Rosenthal and Winkler, 1980).

The last sentence of this letter tacitly recognizes the extreme infrequency of death and explicitly suggests that, for some, death rates are of secondary importance to intervention rates in auditing practice. This emphasis is consistent with the example cited from Oxford at the beginning of this chapter. Many women there had complained about their experiences during labour, in particular that labour had been induced artificially for reasons which they suspected were related to medical convenience. The individual perception of each of these women was probably uninfluenced by the fact that, *as a group*, Oxford women were at exceptionally low *risk* of losing their babies through perinatal death. For any *particular* woman, the outcome was either a live baby or a dead baby.

The relative risk of an Oxford woman losing her baby has remained low over the years since the Oxford Consumer Group's survey in 1973. But by 1979, Kitzinger's *Good Birth Guide* was able to report that the maternity hospital in Oxford was one of the three maternity hospitals in Britain which women had rated as "exceptionally good". These accolades did not result from any spectacular technical achievements in lowering still further the already low risk of perinatal mortality; rather it was because these three hospitals were places "where freedom of choice and respect for the individual is linked with human caring; where one's partner is given a warm welcome, there is opportunity for full discussion concerning medical procedures, support for coping in labour in whatever way one wishes, and where it is accepted that the baby belongs to the parents and is not the property of the hospital'' (Kitzinger, 1979).

Both Kitzinger's survey and that of the Oxford Consumer Group five years earlier had methodological weaknesses. But perhaps they both illustrate how perinatal audit could become liberated from its obsession with death and the problems which such a limited view creates. Individual women have differing needs and expectations of care during pregnancy and childbirth. For example, the vast majority will wish to have a live baby; but there will be a few, including some of those who sought termination unsuccessfully, who may hope their babies will not survive. By contrast, many women (particularly those who recognize themselves to be at high risk) will take steps to avoid having a handicapped child; others will accept the risk (and sometimes the certainty) of bearing a handicapped child rather than countenance termination of pregnancy. Likewise, many parents will accept the relatively high risk of their very low birth-weight infant surviving with a serious handicap; others will not.

Sometimes the opinions of individual women on these and similar issues will conflict with those of individual professionals, and indeed with professional consensus. This is not a reason for ignoring these views. When, as is often the case, there is disagreement at ''expert'' levels about modes of management there seems little place for dogmatism and even more reason to take women's wishes and preferences into account (Lumley, 1979). The extent to which these various needs of individual women are met should become the focus of perinatal audit. The extent to which a range of choices is made available to women is one reflection of the relative power of consumers and professionals in determining the nature of services for childbearing women. In circumstances in which compromises are unavoidable we need to ask ''Who makes the ultimate decisions, and why?'' or, as a recent *Lancet* editorial put it ''Whose baby is it anyway?'' (Lancet, 1980).

References

Baird, D .(1980). Comment In *Perinatal Audit and Surveillance*. Edited by I. Chalmers and G. McIlwaine. London: Royal College of Obstetricians and Gynaecologists.

Baird, D., Walker, J. and Thomson, A. M. (1954). The causes and prevention of stillbirths and first week deaths. *Journal of Obstetrics and Gynaecology of the British Empire*, **61**, 433–448.

Bakketeig, L. S., Hoffmann, H. and Sternthal, P. M. (1978). Obstetric service and perinatal mortality in Norway. *Acta Obstetrica et Gynaecologica Scandinavica Supplement* 77, 3–19.

Banta, H. D. and Thacker, S. B. (1979a). Assessing the costs and benefits of electronic fetal monitoring. *Obstetrical and Gynecological Survey*, **34**, 627–642.

Banta, H. D. and Thacker, S. B. (1979b). Policies toward medical technology: the case of electronic fetal monitoring. *American Journal of Public Health*, **61**, 931–935.

Bardon, D. (1980). Paper prepared for a meeting of the National Childbirth Trust. London, 29th August.

Barron, S. L. (1979). Self-critical analysis. *British Medical Journal*, i, 473–474.

Blunt, V. A. W. (1979). In *Minutes of Evidence to the Expenditure Committee* (Social Services and Employment Sub-Committee). 27th March. London: HMSO.

Chalmers, I. (1976). British debate on obstetric practice. *Pediatrics*, **58**, 308–312.

Chalmers, I. (1979). Randomized controlled trials of intrapartum fetal monitoring 1973–1977. In *Perinatal Medicine*. Edited by O. Thalhammer, K. Baumgarten and A. Pollak, pp. 260–265. Stuttgart: Georg Thieme.

Chalmers, I. and Macfarlane, A. J. (1980). Interpretation of perinatal statistics. In *Topics in Perinatal Medicine*. Edited by B. Wharton, pp. 1–11. Tunbridge Wells: Pitman Medical.

Chalmers, I. and Richards, M. P. M. (1977). Intervention and causal inference in obstetric practice. In *Benefits and Hazards of the New Obstetrics*. Edited by T. Chard and M. P. M. Richards, pp. 34–61. Clinics in Developmental Medicine, No. 64. London: Spastics International Medical Publications/Heinemann Medical Books.

Chalmers, I., Oakley, A. and Macfarlane, J. A. (1980). Perinatal health services: an immodest proposal. *British Medical Journal*, i, 842–845.

Chalmers, T. C. (1974). The impact of controlled trials on the practice of medicine. *Mount Sinai Journal of Medicine*, **41**, 753–759.

Dennis, J. (1978). Neonatal convulsions: aetiology, late neonatal status and long-term outcome. *Developmental Medicine and Child Neurology*, **20**, 143–158.

de Sa, D. (1979). Coronary arterial lesions and myocardial necrosis in stillbirths and infants. *Archives of Diseases in Childhood*, **54**, 918–930.

Diggory, P. (1981). The long-term effects upon the child of perinatal events. In *Changing Patterns of Child Bearing and Child Rearing*, edited by R. Chester, P. Diggory and M. Sutherland. London: Academic Press.

Doughty, A. (1978). Epidural analgesia in labour: the past, the present and the future. *Journal of the Royal Society of Medicine*, **72**, 879–884.

Drillien, C. M. (1978). Aetiology of severely handicapping conditions in early childhood. In *Major Mental Handicap: Methods and Costs of Prevention*. Edited by K. Elliot and M. O'Connor, p. 19. CIBA Foundation Symposium 59 (new series). Amsterdam: Elsevier.

Dyck, F. J., Murphy, F. A., Murphy, J. K., Road, D. A., Boyd, M. S., Osborne, E., de Vlieger, D., Korchinski, B., Ripley, C., Bromley, A. T. and Innes, P. B. (1977). Effect of surveillance on hysterectomies in Saskatchewan. *New England Journal of Medicine*, **296**, 1326–1328.

Farrant, W. (1980). Stress after amniocentesis for high serum alpha-fetoprotein concentrations. *British Medical Journal*, i, 452.

Fox, H. (1978). *Pathology of the Placenta*, p. 258. London: W. B. Saunders.

Friedman, H. S., Chokshi, A. B., Malach, M., Vasavada, B. C. and Bleicher, S. J. (1980). Have pacemakers found their way into too many patients? *Journal of the American Medical Association*, **243**, 2371–2372.

Grimes, D. A. (1977). The impact of state maternal mortality study committees on maternal deaths in the United States. *American Journal of Public Health*, **67**, 830–833.

Hack, M., Demonterice, D., Merkatz, I., Jones, P. and Fanaroff, A. (1981). Re-hospitalization of the very low birthweight infant — a continuum of perinatal and environmental morbidity. *American Journal of Diseases of Children* **135**, 263–266.

Haverkamp, A. D., Thompson, H. E., McFee, J. G. and Cetrulo, C. (1976). The evaluation of continuous fetal heart rate monitoring in high-risk pregnancy. *American Journal of Obstetrics and Gynecology*, **125**, 310–320.

Haverkamp, A. D., Orleans, M., Langendoerfer, S., McFee, J. G., Murphy, J. and Thompson, H. E. (1979). A controlled trial of the differential effects of intrapartum fetal monitoring. *American Journal of Obstetrics and Gynecology*, **134**, 399–412.

Hey, E. (1980). Retrolental fibroplasia as one index of perinatally acquired handicap. In *Perinatal Audit and Surveillance*. Edited by I. Chalmers and G. McIlwaine. London: Royal College of Obstetricians and Gynaecologists.

House of Commons (1980). *Perinatal and Neonatal Mortality*. Second Report from the Social Services Committee, Session 1979–80. Vol. I. *Report*. Cmnd. 663-1. London: HMSO.

Kelso, I. M., Parsons, R. J., Lawrence, G. F., Arora, S. S., Edmonds, D. K. and Cooke, I. D. (1978). An assessment of continuous fetal heart rate monitoring in labor: a randomized trial. *American Journal of Obstetrics and Gynecology*, **131**, 526–532.

Kerr, M. G. (1975). *Problems and Perspectives in Reproductive Medicine*. University of Edinburgh Inaugural Lecture, No. 61.

Kitchen, W. H., Richards, A., Ryan, M. M., McDougall, A. B., Billson, F. A., Kier, E. H. and Naylor, F. D. (1979). A longitudinal study of very low birthweight infants. II. Results of a controlled trial of intensive care and incidence of handicap. *Developmental Medicine and Child Neurology*, **21**, 582–589.

Kitzinger, S. (1979). *The Good Birth Guide*. London: Fontana Paperbacks.

Lancet (1980). Whose baby is it anyway? *Lancet*, *i*, 1326–1328.

Luft, H. A., Bunker, J. P. and Enthoven, A. C. (1979). Should operations be regionalized? *New England Journal of Medicine*, **301**, 1364–1369.

Lumley, J. (1979). Making choices about birth. *Patient Management*, October, 51–55.

Lynch, M. A. and Roberts, J. (1977). Predicting child abuse: signs of bonding failure in the maternity hospital. *British Medical Journal*, *i*, 624–626.

McCarthy, B. J., Terry, J., Rochat, R. W., Quave, S. and Tyler, C. W. (1980). The underregistration of neonatal deaths. *American Journal of Public Health*, **70**, 977–982.

McColl, I., Fernow, L. C., Mackie, C. and Rendall, M. (1976). Communication as a method of medical audit. *Lancet*, *i*, 1341–1344.

Macfarlane, A. J., Chalmers, I. and Adelstein, A. M. (1980). The role of standardisation in the interpretation of perinatal mortality rates. *Health Trends*, **12**, 45–50.

Macfarlane, A. J. (1980). Studies of cerebral palsy. In *Perinatal Audit and Surveillance*. Edited by I. Chalmers and G. McIlwaine. London: Royal College of Obstetricians and Gynaecologists.

McIlwaine, G. M., Howat, R. C. L., Dunn, F. and Macnaughton, M. C. (1979). The Scottish perinatal mortality survey. *British Medical Journal*, *ii*, 1103–1106.

Maclean, U. (1975). Patient delay: some observations on medical claims to certainty. *Lancet*, *ii*, 23–25.

Marieskind, H. (1979). *An Evaluation of Caesarean Section in the United States*. Washington, D.C.: U.S. Department of Health, Education and Welfare.

Medical Research Council (1979). *Report of the MRC Workshop on Perinatology*. Ottawa: Medical Research Council of Canada.

Miller, J. F., Williamson, E., Glue, J., Gordon, Y. B., Grudzinskas, J. G. and Sykes, A. (1980). Fetal loss after implantation. *Lancet*, *ii*, 554–556.

Mitchell, P. and Chalmers, I. (1980). Perinatal practice and compensation for handicap. *British Medical Journal*, **281**, 868.

National Institutes of Health (1979). Report of a task force on predictors of fetal distress. In *Antenatal Diagnosis*, p. 166. Washington, D.C.: U.S. Department of Health, Education and Welfare.

Neldam, S. (1980). Fetal movements as an indicator of fetal wellbeing. *Lancet, i*, 1222–1224.

Newcombe, R. G., Campbell, H. and Chalmers, I. (1975). Maternal deaths. *Lancet, ii*, 1099.

Perry, S. and Kalberer, J. T. (1980). The NIH consensus — development program and the assessment of health-care technologies. *New England Journal of Medicine*, **303**, 169–172.

Renou, P., Chang, A., Anderson, I. and Wood, C. (1976). Controlled trial of fetal intensive care. *American Journal of Obstetrics and Gynecology*, **126**, 470–476.

Richards, G. (1980). Perinatal mortality rates. *British Medical Journal*, **280**, 1622.

Robertson, N. R. C. (1977). Management of neonatal respiratory failure. *Journal of the Royal College of Physicians*, **11**, 389–400.

Robinson, J. (1974). Consumer attitude to maternity care. *Oxford Consumer*, May.

Rosenthal, H. and Winkler, F. (1980). Letter to *The Guardian*, 9th October.

Russell, I. T. and Wilcox, A. J. (1980). *Why Standardize for Birthweight in the Analysis of Perinatal Mortality?* Paper presented at the Annual Meeting of the Society for Social Medicine. Cambridge, 17th–19th September.

Sameroff, A. J. and Chandler, M. J. (1975). Reproductive risk and the continuum of care-taking causality. In *Review of Child Development Research*. Edited by F. D. Horowitz, M. Hetherington, S. Scarr-Salapatek and G. Siegal, Vol. 4, Pt. 4, pp. 187–244. Chicago: University of Chicago Press.

Scanlon, J. W. (1980). One kilogram babies. *Lancet, i*, 655.

Scott, M. J., Ritchie, J. W. K., McClure, B. G., Reid, M. McC. and Halliday, H. (1981). Perinatal death recording: time for a change? *British Medical Journal*, **282**, 707.

Silverman, W. A. (1980). *Retrolental Fibroplasia: A Modern Parable*. Monographs in Neonatology. New York: Grune and Stratton.

Spellacy, W. N., Buhi, W. C. and Birk, S. A. (1975). The effectiveness of human placental lactogen measurements as an adjunct in decreasing perinatal deaths: results of retrospective and randomized controlled prospective study. *American Journal of Obstetrics and Gynecology*, **121**, 835–844.

Stevenson, T. H. C. (1910). Suggested lines of advance in English vital statistics. *Journal of the Royal Statistical Society*, **73**, 685–713.

Wigglesworth, J. S. (1980). Monitoring perinatal mortality: a pathophysiological approach. *Lancet, ii*, 684–686.

Wilkinson, A. R. and Howat, P. (1980). One kilogram babies. *Lancet, i*, 655.

Womersley, J. and MacDonald, I. R. (1980). Implementing a local information service. In *Perinatal Audit and Surveillance*. Edited by I. Chalmers and G. McIlwaine. London: Royal College of Obstetricians and Gynaecologists.

World Health Organization (1978). *International Classification of Diseases*. Ninth Revision. Vol. 1, p. 765. Geneva: World Health Organization.

The Scope of Perinatal Statistics and the Usefulness of International Comparisons

EVA ALBERMAN

Department of Clinical Epidemiology,
The London Hospital Medical College, London

Introduction

Perinatal mortality rates are determined by many different factors, biological, demographic, socio-economic and behavioural. It follows that the scope of perinatal statistics is exceedingly wide, and is becoming wider as we come to learn more of the complicated relationship between the variables.

Overall rates of perinatal mortality can be reduced by a general improvement in the standard of living, which may act directly on parental health, on health behaviour, or by encouraging demographic changes which reduce the size of groups at high risk. Even in the absence of such changes, improvements in medical care, or in its accessibility, can compensate to a large extent for poor social conditions or an unfavourable demographic structure. The expected effect of improvements in medical care would be a reduction in specific immediate causes of death, known to respond to expert treatment. However, for the long term, we need information that will increase our understanding of the underlying causes of all perinatal deaths so that we can prevent these causes from occurring and so reduce the need for medical intervention and avoid the salvage of damaged infants.

Only increasing sophistication in the collection, analysis and comparison of data relating to perinatal risk will provide such information and give us means of measuring how far we are achieving these aims. In the following account the routine data collection and analyses already available in this country and their limitations will be described, as well as the enrichment of our data by the judicious use of international data. Some of the ways in which such data have recently been used in attempts to improve the planning and effectiveness of medical care in reducing perinatal mortality will also be discussed.

Constraints on Routine Data Collection

The constraints on the routine information collected on a national scale lie in the nature, format and quality of the data collected, and in the analyses which are performed and made available. These will vary from country to country, as will the definitions used. With the exception of a few enthusiasts, the medical profession in this and other countries is profoundly uninterested in the question of data collection and tends to be lax and inaccurate in the completion of forms. On the other hand there is a tendency to try to make up for deficiencies in information by producing more and more forms to complete, a reaction which is demonstrably counter-productive. Moreover most doctors, justifiably at present, mistrust the quality of the information produced. This is a vicious circle which needs to be broken before we can obtain the full benefit of our own expensive, and potentially extremely efficient, data collecting and processing organization. The publicizing of the results of data collection, and of analyses useful to the clinician, must be the first stage in achieving this goal.

Enumeration and Description of Births in England and Wales

The actual enumeration and description of births, the essential denominator data for our perinatal death statistics, are based on a dual system of civil birth certification and medical birth notification.

BIRTH AND STILLBIRTH REGISTRATION

The civil registration of births was introduced in 1836 by the first of a series of Marriage and Registration Acts. The current registration of births and deaths is regulated by the 1953 Births and Deaths Registration Act and includes the civil registration of still-births which was first introduced in 1927.

It is primarily the responsibility of the parents to register a birth, within 42 days, with the Registrar of Births and Deaths of the sub-district within which the birth occurred. The registration takes the form of a confidential interview with the parents and the completion of a draft entry. The current regulations prescribe that the following particulars are entered on the entry and in the local register:

(a) the child's date and place of birth, name and surname, and sex;

(b) the name and surname and place of birth of the parents;
(c) the father's occupation;
(d) the mother's maiden surname and, if different, the name in which she married the father of the child;
(e) address of the mother.

Particulars of an illegitimate child's father can be entered in the register only under one of the following conditions:

(a) if the father attends with the mother to give information to the Registrar and also signs the register;
(b) if he acknowledges paternity in a statutory declaration;
(c) if the mother produces an affiliation order naming the father.

At the time of registering a live- or still-birth, the Registrar collects additional confidential information for statistical purposes which is not entered in the register. This comprises: date of birth of mother; date of birth of father if his name is entered in the register; for legitimate children only, the date of the parents' marriage; whether the mother has been married more than once; the number of previous children by her present or any former husband, distinguishing between the number born alive and the number stillborn. The occurrence of a multiple birth is also noted. In the case of still-births, information from the medical certificate of still-births is also entered, naming the cause and giving the duration of pregnancy and birth-weight.

STATISTICAL OUTCOMES OF BIRTH CERTIFICATION

The draft entries of still- or live-births are sent weekly to the Office of Population Censuses and Surveys (OPCS) where they are collected for the whole country. These form the basis of the weekly reports of birth registrations and of the annual reports, giving time of occurrence as well as the usual place of residence of the mother. They form the main statutory source of data available on births on a national scale and the format of the entries dictates the information available on the country's births. Thus social class data and maternal parity data are available only for legitimate births, and length of gestation data only for still-births.

MEDICAL BIRTH NOTIFICATION

Since 1936, the person in attendance upon the mother at the time of, or within six hours after, a birth has been required to notify the fact of the birth to the local health authority, currently through the Area Medical Officer. This person is nearly always a doctor or midwife. Although the format of the notification form is left to the Health Authority, the Department of Health and Social Security (DHSS) have asked that the following items be included: mother's name; date of birth; and, if known, her National Health Service number; her usual address and, if different, the address to which she will proceed immediately after discharge from hospital; date, time and place of birth; live or still-birth; single or multiple birth; period of gestation; mother's previous pregnancies, live or still-birth or miscarriages; sex of baby; birth-weight; nature of any congenital abnormalities observed at birth; name and address of mother's general practitioner.

USES OF BIRTH NOTIFICATION

The main purpose of notification is to provide a means of alerting those responsible for the subsequent care of mother and child. However, information from notification can also be used for statistical and epidemiological purposes. This is particularly important in the case of birth-weight and for the birth prevalence of visible congenital malforma-tions; notification is the only national source of data for both of these.

The DHSS recommends that all Area Health Authorities (AHA) send to the local Registrars of Births and Deaths the following information derived from the notifications: date, time and place of birth; live or still-birth; full name of mother and her postal address; the sex and birth-weight of the baby. In their turn the Registrars are required to furnish to a prescribed medical officer of the corresponding AHA the particulars of each birth and death they have registered. This interchange of information not only provides a cross-check for notifica-tion and registration, but also the opportunity to enter on the birth certificate the birth-weight of the baby, thereby making it accessible to national statistical analysis together with data derived from registration. Unfortunately this transfer is not yet complete: only 78.4% of the birth certificates included birth-weight information in April 1980 (Office of Population Censuses and Surveys, 1980) but renewed efforts are being made to obtain 100% transfer. Very recently I have been informed that this proportion is now over 90% (personal communication, DHSS). Since 1952 local health authorities have been required to send annual returns of numbers of babies weighing 2500 (5½ lbs) or less to the DHSS, classified by weight group, survival, and place of birth, and these data have been published by the DHSS in their annual reports *On the State of Health of the Nation*.

Local health authorities are also asked to provide the DHSS with returns of reported malformations, and these returns act as a warning system for any sudden increases in specific defects. However, they are relevant only for defects visible at birth, which limits their usefulness considerably. This country, together with others from the EEC, is currently studying the possibility of extending such returns to defects diagnosed later in life.

NEONATAL AND LATER INFANT DEATHS

In the United Kingdom the death of a live-born infant, even within minutes of birth, is registered like any other death, and its cause must be certified by a registered medical practitioner on the standard cause of death form based on that recommended by the World Health Organization (WHO). The information asked on cause of death differs somewhat from that asked for still-births since there is no question as to the contribution of maternal factors in the case of deaths of live-births. This detracts considerably from the quality of the information available on the cause of deaths of live-births, as does the absence of information on birth-weight or gestation, or multiple birth, none of which is available on the standard death certificate.

The cause of death is coded at the Office of Population Censuses and Surveys according to the current International Classification of Deaths and Diseases, the Ninth Revision and its conventions being used since 1 January 1979. The cause to which the death is attributed in annual statistics is that said to be underlying, but all other causes given are coded and held for multiple cause analysis, the results of which are not routinely available.

Because of the deficiencies of information available on deaths of live-births, Morris, Heady and their colleagues in the 1950s (Morris and Heady, 1955; Heady and Heasman, 1959) first introduced the idea of linking one year's infant death data with the information available on the corresponding birth certificates so that these deaths could be related to denominator data for maternal age, parity, social class, marital status and place of residence and compared with these parameters in live-births. A similar exercise was carried out by Spicer and Lipworth (1966) in 1964, and since 1975 birth and infant death data have been linked routinely. The most recent report of the results of linkage was by Adelstein and his colleagues (1980) and, for the first time, information was included on mortality by mother's place of birth, perinatal mortality by place of birth, and perinatal mortality of multiple births.

HOSPITAL STATISTICS

National Health Service hospitals including maternity units are required to collect annual statistics of two main types to return to the DHSS. The first is in the Series SH3, where the hospital is asked to provide returns of available beds and their use, annual numbers of births and still-births, and antenatal attendances. The second is in the series required by the Hospital In-patient Enquiry (HIPE) and includes data on maternity bed use, use of Special Care cots, complications arising from pregnancy and delivery, and some data on the outcome of pregnancy (Ashley, 1980). It is from these data that information on such factors as rates of caesarean section, induction of labour, and incidence of episiotomy on a national scale is available. DHSS manpower statistics also include data on the number of doctors of different grades working in obstetrics and gynaecology, and the number of midwives. Tables from HIPE also give information on the use of hospital beds, and provide such data as mean length of antenatal and post-natal stay. Recently such data for the years 1973 to 1976 have been collected together and published in the Series MB4 (Department of Health and Social Security and Office of Population Censuses and Surveys, 1980).

Although these data can act as a guide to the current situation, we lack validation of the quality of data obtained in this way. For instance there is some doubt about the way in which the word "induction" is interpreted. Manpower statistics are very difficult to interpret when doctors attend several different hospitals or when midwives are shared between the hospital and the community, and crude numbers of clinic attendances are not very informative. Scotland is more advanced than England and Wales in this respect, and has better designed and validated data of this type (Cole, 1980).

DATA ANALYSIS AND PRESENTATION

Recently there has been a development and improvement of methods of analysing and presenting these and corresponding data collected by other countries to try to distinguish between the role of medical care in reducing mortality and that of social, behavioural and demographic factors; there has also been an attempt to relate outcome to medical care resources. Such analyses largely depend on comparisons between perinatal outcomes, allowing for factors other than medical care.

CROSS-SECTIONAL "PROFILES" OF BIRTHS AND THEIR RELATIONSHIP TO PERINATAL DEATHS

The first step in such analyses is to present for the populations under study a profile, as comprehensive as possible, of the demographic, social and biological characteristics of their births. To be useful this must be given in a standard and comparable format. While this is possible within countries, between country comparisons may be bedevilled by differences in definition or interpretation, such as for occupational groups, or even by the different grouping of variables, for example birth-weight or maternal age.

REGIONAL COMPARISONS

The linked file system now in routine use at OPCS is making it possible to provide regular tabulations by each Health Authority for England and Wales, which goes a considerable way towards producing regular "profiles" of births. An example of such tabulations of perinatal mortality by distributions of single variables is given in Tables I to III which compare the births in 1978 in the Northern Regional Health Authority (RHA) with those of the East Anglian RHA (OPCS 1980). These show how the higher mortality in the Northern RHA is in part accounted for by its larger proportion of certain high risk groups, particularly teenage mothers, Social Class V and, independently of the latter, illegitimate births. Over and above these demographic differences the subgroups themselves frequently have a higher perinatal mortality in the Northern than in the East Anglian RHA.

Table I
Maternal age distribution and perinatal mortality rate per 1000 total births in the Northern and East Anglia RHAs 1978

Maternal Age	RHA				
	Northern		East Anglian		
	%	PNMR	%	PNMR	
under 16	0.2	(small nos)	0.2	(small nos)	
16–19	11.3	25	7.7	21	
20–24	34.2	16	31.5	13	
25–29	33.9	16	37.1	11	
30–34	15.8	15	18.8	11	
35 and over	4.6	29	4.7	23	

Table II
Social class distribution and perinatal mortality rate per 1000 total births in the Northern and East Anglia RHAs 1978

Social Class	RHA Northern %	RHA Northern PNMR	East Anglian %	East Anglian PNMR
I	6.5	11	9.0	11
II	15.9	14	21.1	13
III	52.3	18	48.8	11
IV	16.9	16	18.1	13
V	8.4	18	3.1	31

Table III
Illegitimacy distribution and perinatal mortality rate per 1000 total births in the Northern and East Anglia RHAs 1978

Legitimacy	RHA Northern %	RHA Northern PNMR	East Anglian %	East Anglian PNMR
Legitimate	89.4	16	92.2	13
Illegitimate	10.6	27	7.8	13

The DHSS also provides some data on birth-weight distribution by each RHA, from which we know that the proportion of babies of low birth-weight is higher in the Northern RHA than in East Anglia. In 1978 the proportion of total notified births was 6.4% in the Northern, but 5.9% in the East Anglian RHA (personal communication, DHSS). The latter difference is almost certainly associated with the demography of births in the two Regions, and it is still a serious gap in OPCS data that we are not able to relate birth-weight distribution to other "profile" data. Birth-weight data by Health Authority is not systematically published, but was last made available by Region in the *OPCS Monitors*, Series DH3, for 1979. Chalmers and his colleagues (1978) (Table IV) and later Mallett and Knox (1979) showed how standardization to allow for differences in birth-weight distribution can substantially change the ranking order of perinatal mortality in different Area Health Authorities.

A recent WHO study (1978), in which the presentation of largely routinely collected national data from eight countries was made in a

Table IV
Ranking of crude and birth-weight adjusted perinatal mortality rate in Areas in the N.E. Thames RHA (Chalmers et al., 1978)

Area Health Authority	Crude PNMR	1976 Rank order	PNMR adjusted for proportion of infants under 2000g	Rank order
City and East London	19.1	1	17.0	5
Enfield and Haringey	18.8	2	18.7	1
Barking and Havering	17.0	3	18.0	2
Redbridge and Waltham Forest	16.5	4	17.6	3
Essex	15.8	5	17.3	4
Camden and Islington	11.0	6	10.5	6

standard format, provided an example of the considerable usefulness of international comparisons when properly conducted. This gave tabulations similar to those above but with the addition of birth-weight data for countries other than England and Wales. These data confirm the importance of demographic and biological differences in accounting for some of the differences in perinatal mortality observed between countries (Table V). The use of standardization techniques makes it possible to quantify the size of some of these individual effects, and to show how allowing for differences in birth-weight can change the ranking order of perinatal mortality levels of different countries (Table VI).

Similar calculations have been used to estimate the proportion of the improvement in mortality rate occurring between 1950 to 1973 in England and Wales due to changes in the maternal age, parity and social class distribution (Hellier, 1977), and between 1953 to 1975 in Sweden for maternal age and parity only (Meirik et al., 1979). Hellier found that a quarter of the improvement that had occurred in England and Wales could be explained by advantageous changes in these demographic characteristics but Meirik and his colleagues found that only 9 per cent of the improvement in Swedish rates could be explained thus. Hellier (quoted by Alberman, 1979) used the same method to show that in 1973 differences in perinatal mortality rate in 8 out of 15 Regions could be "explained by differences in social class, maternal age and parity structure but these would not explain the remaining differences or the extremes observed".

Eventually such birth profiles should be improved further by the routine addition of such factors as birth-weight, the proportion

Table V

Parity 4+, teenage pregnancy, % low birth-weight and perinatal mortality in selected countries (1973)

	% births parity 4 +	% births to mothers under 20	% births 2500g or less	perinatal mortality per 1000 total births
Sweden	1.8	7.5	3.9	12.6
USA (part)	9.7	17.6	6.0	14.9
Japan	0.8	0.9	5.3	17.0
New Zealand (legit only)	7.6	14.6	5.2	17.3
England and Wales (legit only)	3.9	11.0	not available for report	18.9
Austria	7.7	14.5	5.7	21.4
Cuba	17.7	22.3	10.8	26.9
Hungary	4.1	16.5	10.8	29.1

Source: WHO Report on *Social and Biological Effects on Perinatal Mortality* (1978) Vol. 1, Tables 5.4, 5.5 and p. 53.

Table VI

Crude and birth-weight adjusted perinatal mortality rate in selected countries 1973

	Crude rates	Rank order	Standardized rates	Rank order
Hungary	29.1	1	16.6	5
Cuba	26.9	2	20.1	1
Austria	21.4	3	18.2	3
New Zealand	17.3	4	17.3	4
Japan	17.0	5	18.9	2
United States (part)	14.9	6	11.7	7
Sweden	12.6	7	14.5	6

Source: WHO Report on *Social and Biological Effects on Perinatal Mortality* (1978) Vol. 1, p. 54.

of mothers of different ethnic groups and those with multiple births.

THE ROLE OF MEDICAL CARE IN THE REDUCTION OF PERINATAL MORTALITY

As was said earlier, these reports are basically an attempt to separate out the effects on perinatal mortality of factors intrinsic to the mother and child from those of extrinsic factors such as medical care. Such calculations can do no more than indicate an upper limit on the possible effect of the latter factors. In order to get a better estimate it is necessary to look at the perinatal outcome of births of comparable "profile" who have received different types of medical care. The best method to adopt for such studies would be the randomized control trial. As Dr. Chalmers stated earlier, specific forms of management of obstetric care, such as fetal monitoring, have now been subjected to such trials, largely with equivocal results. Routinely collected data do give some opportunity to study the effect of medical care but this is as yet another under-developed area in perinatal research, and it has already been indicated that the quality of data routinely collected on the management of labour is not sufficiently good to use for this purpose.

One study of the effect of the resource level of medical care, which could easily be repeated on a national scale, was that reported by Bakketeig *et al.* from Norway (1978) who showed that, after allowing for birth-weight, groups of institutions with the most generous obstetric, paediatric, anaesthetic and laboratory facilities had the lowest perinatal mortality rates.

A crude study of outcome in institutions of different size can present some indication of the effect of medical care. The recent report by the Social Services Committee (1980; see Table VII) showed how still-birth rate in different institutions varied with the number of births occurring each year, and suggested that the rise in rate from the very busiest units to the smaller consultant units might reflect levels of staffing. Unfortunately in England and Wales there is as yet no means of using the demographic or birth-weight profile for births in different institutions to refine such interpretations, and this is another gap in our statistical data collection.

Table VII
Still-birth rates in Consultant Obstetric Units with different numbers of deliveries in 1978 (House of Commons, 1980)

Number deliveries/year	Still-birth rates 1978 Consultant Units + GP beds	Consultant Units
50-	—	1.3
200-	2.1	4.6
500-	3.5	7.7
1000-	8.8	9.0
2000-	8.9	8.8
3000-	9.3	9.2
4000-	8.4	8.9

Chalmers (1979) has pointed out that another important defect of our present attempts to evaluate the effect of medical care is our dependence on perinatal death as a measure of outcome. In the long term we will need to develop far more sensitive measures, based on morbidity rather than mortality.

LONGITUDINAL STUDIES OF REPRODUCTIVE HISTORY

Although cross-sectional profiles are quite adequate for the purposes that have been described, it is becoming increasingly clear that to identify the basic causes that predispose a woman to reproductive failure we need to look at reproductive history longitudinally within women. Bakketeig and Hoffman (1979) have made very good use of a unique data base available in Norway where births to the same mother are linked together by an identifying number. They have shown that the J-shaped pattern of risk seen in cross-sectional studies of births of different birth-order is an artefact due to the consistently higher perinatal mortality rates at all birth orders of women who have large numbers of pregnancies. They have also demonstrated again the tendency of mothers to repeat similar birth-weight–gestation patterns which, amongst other things, tends to militate against rapid changes in national birth-weight and gestation distribution (Bakketeig *et al.*, 1979).

In this country we have made a beginning on the collection of such a data base with the OPCS cohort study linking events such as births and deaths for a 1% sample of the population chosen for their date of birth. As yet the numbers are too small to produce any data comparable with those of the Norwegians.

Causes of Perinatal Death

It might be thought that much of the evaluative work described above would be better carried out using specific causes of death as an outcome. However the usual way in which cause of death is presented is of little use for such studies, based as it is only on the underlying immediate cause of death, without taking into account maternal and fetal predisposing factors. In the diagram of underlying cause of perinatal death given in Fig. 1, actual birth-weight is not taken into account, nor is the fact of multiple birth acknowledged where it is not given as a cause of death. Even the "prem." category which includes

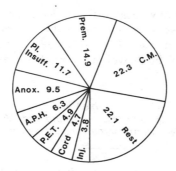

FIG. 1. Percentage distribution of major underlying certified cause of death derived from "P" list of IC classification — England and Wales, 1978 (Office of Population Censuses and Surveys, 1980)

all the codes labelled as immaturity does not include all low birth-weight deaths, for these may be included under multiple birth, congenital malformations or even birth injury. Conversely the cause of death of some multiple births may be allocated to the immaturity group. Although there are coding conventions to direct such classifications these depend on what is actually written on the certificate, by doctors who have usually had no training in the classification of deaths. Information on birth-weight included in the cause of death coding has recently been presented for the first time (OPCS, 1981) and helps enormously in the interpretation of the reports for planning purposes.

Moreover, as was pointed out earlier, the death certificate for still-births differs from that for neonatal deaths so that one would expect to find differences in certified causes between still-births and neonatal deaths, even though the basic aetiology might have been the same.

However, the study of data as currently presented does reveal that sustained improvements over recent years have been most marked in the categories due to difficult labour, haemolytic disease of the newborn, pre-eclampsia and placental haemorrhage (Edouard and Alberman, 1980). As one would expect, they have been least marked for congenital malformations although, even for these, there has been a fall. This brings up the important point that one really needs data on the incidence of complications as well as on mortality. One might expect to find medical care reducing fatality rate from specific causes rather than reducing the incidence of these causes, whilst environmental improvements should affect incidence rather than fatality. For most causes there are few data on incidence over time. A good example of a situation where we have data is low birth-weight, and Tables VIII and IX show that whereas there has been very little change in the incidence of very low birth-weight over the years, fatality has fallen sharply.

Table VIII
Mortality rates: births of 1000g or less — England and Wales 1965/66 and 1976/77
(derived from Pharoah and Alberman, 1980)

	1965/66	1976/77
% births ≤ 1000g	0.424	0.353
SB/1000 total births	401.5	352.7
Day 0 deaths/1000 LB	651.0	542.9
Day 1–28 deaths/1000 survivors	569.8	472.4
% SB + NND all weights	13.6	16.2

Table IX
Mortality rates: births of 1001–1500g — England and Wales 1965/66 and 1976/77
(derived from Pharoah and Alberman, 1980)

	1965/66	1976/77
% births 1001–1500g	0.671	0.643
SB/1000 TB	360.5	276.8
Day 0 deaths/1000 LB	306.7	195.6
Day 1–28	249.8	169.6
% SB + NND all weights	15.8	18.0

The problems of international comparisons of cause of death were emphasized by the WHO report (1978). One problem already discussed above in relation to still-birth and neonatal death certification was that in a country such as New Zealand, where there is a special section on the death certificate for maternal causes, the latter tend to be reported more frequently than in countries where there is no such section. This and other differences in certifying habits make it very difficult to compare crude tabulations of underlying causes. Differences in demography also add to this problem. As the WHO report showed, certain causes, such as placenta praevia and premature separation, rose with increasing parity in most participating countries. The problem of distinguishing between incidence and case fatality also rises in international comparisons. For example, although Sweden has a much lower incidence rate of low birth-weight than England and

Wales, the case fatality for the lowest birth-weight group is sometimes higher (Table X) (Adelstein, 1978).

Table X
Low Birth-weight specific mortality rates: England and Sweden 1971 (Adelstein, 1978)

Birth-weight (g)	England Neonatal death rate	Sweden Early neonatal death rate
≤ 1000	799.7	873.9
1001–1500	436.8	429.3
1501–2000	139.7	143.4
2001–2500	31.2	31.1
% births between 1001–2500	6.4	3.9

LONG-TERM FOLLOW-UP

Of increasing importance in these days of rapidly falling rates is some means of following up and assessing the health of survivors of a stormy perinatal history such as that of very low birth-weight. In this country, with the NHS covering virtually the whole population, this is in theory a feasible operation and it is being carried out by individual hospitals. Hagberg and his colleagues (1975) have been reporting the results of monitoring the incidence of cerebral palsy in Gothenburg, Sweden, for many years now, and found a fall in the rate of spastic diplegia from 1950 to the mid-1960s in infants of very low birth-weight. This fall levelled out at the end of the 1960s and is possibly being followed by a slight rise in the 1970s (Hagberg, personal communication). Similar studies with different patterns of morbidity have been reported from Australia (Stanley, 1979) and Ireland (Cussen et al., 1979). International comparisons of such data also, if carefully carried out, could point to important differences in outcome with different management.

OTHER STATISTICS OF RELEVANCE TO PERINATAL MORTALITY

There are many other statistics, some already collected, some collected by ad hoc studies from time to time, which would be of relevance. Examples are data on smoking habits of young women, on rubella immunization rates, on attendance at antenatal clinics, prenatal screening, and anti D prophylaxis. Perinatal care has become almost a microcosm of the whole of preventive medicine and these wider aspects cannot be covered here. However such data are of considerable importance in evaluating and planning for perinatal care, and may be of vital importance when international comparisons are carried out.

Conclusion

I have attempted to show the breadth of information now required for an evaluation of perinatal care, and for planning for further reductions in rate of mortality and in improvements in the health of survivors. We are now beyond the stage where simple trends of mortality rates, nationally or internationally, are enough for this purpose. New developments in the collection and analysis of relevant statistics are demanding but rewarding, and will pay for themselves if used intelligently by planners and clinicians.

References

Adelstein, A. M. (1978). Current vital statistics: methods and interpretation. *British Medical Journal*, *ii*, 983–987.

Adelstein, A. M., MacDonald Davies, I. M. and Weatherall, J. A. C. (1980). *Perinatal and Infant Mortality: Social and Biological Factors 1975–1977*. Studies on Medical and Population Subjects, No. 41. London: HMSO.

Alberman, E. (1979). Social and biological effects on perinatal mortality. *Journal of the Royal Society of Medicine*, **72**, 295–297.

Ashley, J. S. A. (1980). The maternity hospital in-patient enquiry. In *Perinatal Audit and Surveillance*. Edited by I. Chalmers and G. McIlwaine. London: Royal College of Obstetricians and Gynaecologists.

Bakketeig, L. S. and Hoffman, H. J. (1979). Perinatal mortality by birth order within cohorts based on sibship size. *British Medical Journal*, *ii*, 693–696.

Bakketeig, L. S., Hoffman, H. J. and Sternthal, P. M. (1978). Obstetric service and perinatal mortality in Norway. *Acta Obstetrica et Gynecologica Scandinavica Supplement* 77, 3–19.

Bakketeig, L. S., Hoffman, H. J. and Harley, E. E. (1979). The tendency to repeat gestational age and birthweight in successive births. *American Journal of Obstetrics and Gynecology*, **135**, 1086–1103.

Chalmers, I. (1979). The search for indices. *Lancet*, *ii*, 1063–1065.

Chalmers, I., Newcombe, R., West, R., Campbell, H., Weatherall, J., Lambert, P. and Adelstein, A. M. (1978). Adjusted perinatal mortality rates in administrative areas of England and Wales. *Health Trends*, **10**, 24–29.

Cole, S. (1980). Scottish maternity and neonatal records. In *Perinatal Audit and Surveillance*. Edited by I. Chalmers and G. McIlwaine. London: Royal College of Obstetricians and Gynaecologists.

Cussen, G. H., Barry, J. E., Moloney, A. M., Buckley, N. M., Crawley, M. and Daly, C. (1979). Cerebral palsy — a regional study. Part II. *Journal of the Irish Medical Association*, **72**, 14–18.

Department of Health and Social Security and Office of Population Censuses and Surveys (1980). *Hospital In-Patient Enquiry*. Maternity Tables 1973–1976, England and Wales. (Series MB4, No. 8). London: HMSO.

Edouard, L. and Alberman, E. (1980). National trends in the certified causes of perinatal mortality: 1968 to 1978. *British Journal of Obstetrics and Gynaecology*, **87**, 833–838.

Hagberg, B., Hagberg, G. and Olow, I. (1975). The changing panorama of cerebral palsy in Sweden, 1954–1970. I. Analysis of the general changes. *Acta Paediatrica Scandinavica*, **64**, 187.

Heady, J. A. and Heasman, M. A. (1959). *Social and Biological Factors in Infant Mortality*. Studies on Medical and Population Subjects, No. 15. London: HMSO.

Hellier, J. (1977). Perinatal mortality, 1950 and 1973. *Population Trends*, **9**, 13–15.

House of Commons (1980). *Perinatal and Neonatal Mortality*. Second Report from the Social Services Committee, Session 1979–80. Vol. I. *Report*, p. 124. Cmnd. 663–1. London: HMSO.

Mallet, R. and Knox, E. G. (1979). Standardised perinatal mortality ratios: technique, utility and interpretation. *Community Medicine*, **1**, 6–13.

Meirik, O., Smedby, B. and Ericson, A. (1979). Impact of changing age and parity distributions of mothers on perinatal mortality in Sweden, 1953–1975. *International Journal of Epidemiology*, **8**, 361–364.

Morris, J. M. and Heady, J. A. (1955). Social and biological factors in infant mortality, I. *Lancet*, *i*, 343.

Office of Population Censuses and Surveys (1980). *Monitors*. London: HMSO.

Pharoah, P. O. D. and Alberman, E. (1980). Mortality of low birthweight infants in England and Wales, 1953–1977. *Archives of Diseases of Childhood*, **56**, 86–89.

Spicer, C. C. and Lipworth, L. (1966). *Regional and Social Factors in Infant Mortality*. Studies on Medical and Population Subjects, No. 19. London: HMSO.

Stanley, F. (1979). An epidemiological study of cerebral palsy in Western Australia, 1956–1975. I. Changes in total incidence of cerebral palsy and associated factors. *Developmental Medicine and Child Neurology*, **21**, 701–713.

World Health Organisation (1978). *Report on Social and Biological Effects on Perinatal Mortality*, Volume 1. Budapest: Statistical Publishing House.

Changing Patterns of Physical Development and Health in Children

W. A. MARSHALL

*Department of Human Sciences, University of Technology, Loughborough
Leicestershire, England*

Today, many children in the more prosperous parts of the world enjoy much better health and nutrition than a hundred years ago. They have become taller and heavier than those of the same age in the past. However, when we enquire into the precise nature of the changes which have taken place and into their causes we become much less certain of our ground. We may find that information which has been taken to represent a given country is in fact derived from only one region of that country. Alternatively, we may find data which are genuinely national but, by virtue of this fact, conceal variation between one part of the nation and another. Also, we may find it difficult to justify a belief that some beneficial changes in the health and development of children are actually the result of medical or social advances.

It is true that, in countries such as ours, the number of children who die before their first birthdays has been reduced to about one-tenth of the corresponding number at the beginning of the century. Nevertheless we still lose about 15 out of every 1000 live-born children in this period. The greater part of the improvement in survival has been due to a reduction in fatal infections such as gastro-enteritis after the perinatal period.

In later childhood, deaths from the hitherto common infections such as measles, whooping cough, etc. are now rare. Diphtheria and poliomyelitis have been virtually eliminated from most of the well-developed countries although they still persist in some areas of southern Europe. Immunization may have played some part in bringing about this improvement although the mortality from tuberculosis, whooping cough and measles had already declined before immunization was introduced. Scarlet fever, which is practically unknown today, was the principal cause of death amongst infectious diseases of childhood during the last century. However, its incidence had begun to decline long before antibiotics became available as an effective weapon against the haemolytic streptococcus. Smallpox has disappeared from most parts of the world.

Mortality is now relatively low between the ages of 1 and 15 years. The number of deaths is about one-third as great as that in the first year alone, however it still amounts to between 5000 and 6000 each year in Scotland, England and Wales. About a quarter of the deaths occurring between 1 and 5 years are due to injury, followed, in order of frequency, by congenital anomalies, respiratory infection and neoplastic disease. Between 5 and 15 years, the number of deaths is about the same as it is between 1 and 5 years but injury accounts for about two-thirds of them. The next most common cause is neoplastic disease whilst respiratory infection moves to third place.

Violence, whether accidental or deliberate, is also a common cause of admission to hospital amongst surviving children and accounted for 16% of hospital discharges in the 0 to 14 age range in 1974, whereas infectious diseases accounted for only 5 per cent.

Non-accidental injury has been drawn increasingly to our attention in recent years and is certainly an important cause of suffering though it is difficult to know how the situation today compares with that in the past. It has been estimated by the British Paediatric Association (1972) that about 2000 cases of child abuse occur each year whilst, in 1973, 61 children were murdered. Clearly, if we wish to increase the survival rate and happiness of our children then research into the prevention of both accidental and non-accidental injury is a matter of priority.

The changing pattern of childhood mortality over the past century has been associated not only with immunization and antibiotics but also with the falling birth rate, together with improvement in housing, sanitation, nutrition, and, possibly above all, better education of mothers. All of these, together with unknown factors, may have contributed to reducing the number of deaths from infectious disease. Nevertheless such diseases still exist, and in various forms, particularly as they affect the respiratory system, remain important causes of illness and distress which is sometimes serious.

In association with the changes in general health and survival which we have discussed above, the average stature of children at all ages has increased dramatically in developed countries. According to Meredith (1976) the secular trend in stature between approximately 1860 and 1960 can be generalized at about 1.3 cm per decade during childhood; increasing to 1.9 cm at age 12 in girls and at age 14 in boys but declining again to only 0.6 cm per decade in adults. The increased difference between the children of today and those of the past at about ages 12 to 14 presumably reflects the earlier occurrence of the adolescent growth spurt in the former group. In other words, modern children would be growing very quickly at ages when the children of a century ago were still growing slowly at pre-adolescent rates. The later adolescent spurt in the past would then reduce the difference at later ages.

The generalization quoted above may or may not accurately describe the situation. It is derived from the total changes which have occurred over a long period of time in a variety of countries and whereas the estimates of total change may be reasonably reliable there is little justification for the assumption that the change has occurred uniformly throughout the century. Indeed, according to Brundtland et al. (1980) the statures of 8 to 14 year old boys and girls in Oslo increased by about 4 cm per decade between 1920 and 1940. A drop of about 1.5 cm occurred during World War II followed by a rapid increase. Since 1950 height has increased only moderately. Another interesting example of failure of stature to increase uniformly over consecutive decades is provided by Polish children in 1932 and 1951 (Mydlarski, 1934 and Trzesniowski, 1961, cited by Malina, 1979). Up to the age of 14 years, the 1951 children were shorter than those of the same age in 1932. Only after the age of 15 were the 1951 children appreciably taller. Presumably all the children measured in 1951 had suffered the deprivation of the Second World War in Poland but those aged 15 or more were born not later than 1936, i.e. three years before the war began. All the younger children would have spent the first three years of their lives in wartime conditions. This suggests that children's future growth may have been particularly sensitive to adverse influences during early childhood. However, a number of unknown local factors may have been responsible for the result in this case. Usually, children whose growth is temporarily impaired by adverse circumstances demonstrate catch-up growth when circumstances improve so that their stature returns to approximately the level it would have reached had the setback not occurred.

It is interesting that, in spite of their shorter statures, the Polish children studied in 1951 showed better performances in running, jumping and throwing than those studied before the war. This implies that impaired growth in stature may not necessarily be accompanied by impairment in general performance and raises the question of whether the delay in growth and maturation which occurs during adversity might be regarded as a useful adaptation rather than an impairment. Time does not permit further discussion at this point.

Tanner (1962) drew attention to the decreasing age of menarche in various populations. This too has been regarded as a fairly uniform process in developed countries where it has apparently progressed at a rate of about four months per decade over the last hundred years or so. However, Brundtland and Walløe (1976) have re-examined the evidence relating to Norway and have concluded that the rate of change was not constant. They suggest that from about 1820 until about 1920 the age of menarche remained fairly constant at about 14 years for the upper and 16 years for the lower social classes. It then decreased to about 13 years in the early fifties. In some of the more prosperous communities the trend towards earlier menarche has apparently stopped. Data from London (Tanner, 1973) and Oslo (Brundtland and Walløe, 1973) indicate that there has been little change in the past ten years or more. The trend may have stopped even earlier in parts of the United States (Maresh, 1972; Damon, 1974). It is important to recognize, however, that the fact that the trend has ceased in the capital city of a country, or in another prosperous area, need not imply that this has occurred over the country as a whole. There may well be many areas in the United Kingdom, Norway, and the United States where the trend towards early menarche is still continuing and where the mean age at menarche is below that reported from more prosperous regions. The trend towards earlier menarche may also be continuing throughout some highly developed countries.

Another change which has apparently taken place in the United Kingdom over recent years is an increase in the number of obese children as indicated by measurement of the subscapular and triceps skinfolds. Centile charts for these parameters produced by Tanner and Whitehouse in 1962 may be compared with those produced by the same authors in 1975. The 50th centiles for both skinfolds have increased only slightly but the 97th centiles have increased throughout childhood and adolescence whilst the third centiles remain essentially unchanged. This evidence that overnutrition has become an important form of malnutrition in some areas should not conceal the fact that there may be many groups of children within this country whose nutrition is still sub-optimal.

In general the data from the more prosperous parts of the world indicate that progress is being made towards optimal health and nutrition for children. However we must recognize that data from major cities, or national averages, do not necessarily reveal important regional variations or differences between other sub-groupings in the population. It is important that these differences should be monitored carefully.

Many of the so-called developing countries present quite a different picture from that described above, as the two intractable problems of nutritional deficiency and infectious disease still result in high mortality and morbidity. Not only does malnutrition increase the likelihood and severity of infection but, conversely, infection predisposes to malnutrition. This interaction is largely responsible for a death rate of about 50 per thousand children under five in many developing countries, i.e. about ten times that in more prosperous parts of the world (Morley, 1973). Gastro-enteritis remains an important cause of death and is apparently more common in those areas where bottle feeding has become fashionable.

The incidence of measles and whooping cough remains high in developing countries and is associated with high mortality. A mortality from measles of 12 per cent has been reported in West Africa (Morley et al., 1966). Malaria, tuberculosis and the common anaemias persist as causes of death and chronic ill-health. Again we should note that these statements are generalizations and subject to considerable regional variation.

There is little evidence as to whether the statures of children in most developing countries are showing the increase which we have observed in other parts of the world but there appears to be little or no change in adult stature in several areas of Asia, Africa and Latin America (Eveleth et al., 1974; Himes and Malina, 1975; Tobias, 1975; Himes and Mueller, 1977). In many populations in India, adult stature may actually be decreasing (Ganguly, 1979).

The sub-optimal state of health and nutrition in parts of many developing countries is associated with short stature in the children. Figure 1, which is based on data from a variety of sources summarized by Eveleth and Tanner (1976), illustrates how the average heights of children at different ages vary in a number of populations. It might be tempting to regard these differences as racial rather than environmental in origin but it is unlikely that this assumption would be more than partially justified. It is probably more correct to regard the differences as reflecting the distinct environmental circumstances of the various samples. For example, children of mainly African ancestry living in Kingston, Jamaica, are as tall as British children whilst those of similar ancestry living in St. Vincent are not. Even in Jamaica, rural children may have relatively short statures (Marshall et al., 1970). It therefore seems likely that some groups of children in the West Indies have not yet undergone an increase in stature comparable with that observed in many parts of Europe and elsewhere, whilst their more privileged peers have done so.

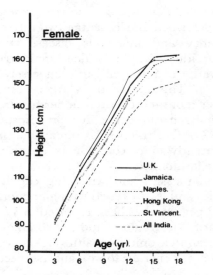

FIG. 1. Mean statures of children (female), according to age, in various populations. Data from Eveleth and Tanner (1976).

The mean statures observed in the all India survey are very small. However the mean value, taken by itself, conceals the wide variation in stature between the distinct cultural groups which inhabit different parts of the Indian sub-continent and who seldom inter-marry. Also, in a country where poverty is widespread, the mean stature gives no indication of the growth potential of children living in favourable circumstances. Apparently well-off Indian boys have statures similar to those of London boys, at least up to the age of about 14 years although they may be relatively shorter at later ages (Raghavan *et al.*, 1971).

Children of Indian ancestry who live in other parts of the world frequently exhibit statures greater than those found in the all India study. The obvious explanation for this, that their families have migrated into better economic circumstances with better nutrition and medical care, may be largely true but does not necessarily reflect the whole truth. The mean statures of populations in different parts of the Indian sub-continent vary greatly, and the taller groups may have migrated in proportionately greater numbers than those with smaller statures. It is not yet clear to what extent the short statures of the inhabitants of some areas of India and neighbouring countries are genetically determined and to what extent they reflect environments which are incompatible with the realization of an existing genetic potential for further growth.

The study of groups of children whose forebears of various races have migrated from one country to another in the past few generations may not only yield useful information about current trends in the health and growth of the migrant groups but indicate what action may be necessary to ensure that future trends are beneficial in both the migrant and the parent communities.

This short paper has dealt only superficially with a few selected aspects of a very complex subject. In general we may conclude that trends towards improvement in the health and development of children are taking place in many populations but are scarcely discernable in others. We cannot assume that all future changes will be favourable, particularly in communities subjected to cultural upheaval or those living near subsistence level. For them a minor change in economic, political or climatic conditions may have far-reaching effects. This applies as much to those children of developed countries whose social position renders them particularly vulnerable to economic recession as to those children who live in areas where poverty is more widely apparent.

References

British Paediatric Association (1972). *Paediatrics in the Seventies*. Edited by D . Court and A. Jackson. Oxford: Oxford University Press.

Brundtland, G. H. and Walløe, L. (1973). Menarcheal age in Norway: halt in the trend towards earlier maturation. *Nature*, **241**, 478–479.

Brundtland, G. H. and Walløe, L. (1976). Menarcheal age in Norway in the nineteenth century: a re-evaluation of the historical sources. *Annals of Human Biology*, **3**, 363–374.

Brundtland, G. H., Liestøl, K. and Walløe, L. (1980). Height, weight and menarcheal age of Oslo schoolchildren during the last sixty years. *Annals of Human Biology*, **7**, 307–322.

Damon, A. (1974). Larger body size and earlier menarche: the end may be in sight. *Social Biology*, **21**, 8–11.

Eveleth, P. B. and Tanner, J. M. (1976). *Worldwide Variation in Human Growth*. Cambridge: Cambridge University Press.

Eveleth, P. B., Salzano, F. M. and de Lima, P. E. (1974). Child growth and adult physique in Brazilian Xingu Indians. *American Journal of Physical Anthropology*, **41**, 95–102.

Ganguly, P. (1979). Progressive decline in stature in India: a study of sixty population groups. In *Physiological and Morphological Adaptation and Evolution*, edited by W. A. Stini. The Hague: Mouton.

Himes, J. H. and Malina, R. M. (1975). Age and secular factors in the stature of adult Zapotec males. *American Journal of Physical Anthropology*, **43**, 367–369.

Himes, J. H. and Mueller, W. M. (1977). Ageing and secular change in adult stature in rural Colombia. *American Journal of Physical Anthropology*, **46**, 275–279.

Malina, R. M. (1979). Secular changes in growth, maturation and physical performance. *Exercise and Sports Sciences Reviews*, **6**, 203–255.

Maresh, M. (1972). A forty-five year investigation for secular changes in physical maturation. *American Journal of Physical Anthropology*, **36**, 103–109.

Marshall, W. A., Ashcroft, M. T. and Bryan, G. (1970). Skeletal maturation of the hand and wrist in Jamaican children. *Human Biology*, **42**, 419–435.

Meredith, H. V. (1976). Findings from Asia, Australia, Europe and North America on secular change in mean height of children, youths and young adults. *American Journal of Physical Anthropology*, **44**, 315–325.

Morley, D. C. (1973). *Paediatric Priorities in the Developing World*. London: Butterworth.

Morley, D. C., Martin, W. J. and Allen, I. (1966). Measles in West Africa. *West African Medical Journal*, **16**, 24–30.

Raghavan, K. V., Singh, D. and Swaminathan, M. C. (1971). Heights and weights of well-nourished Indian children. *Indian Journal of Medical Research*, **59**, 648–654.

Tanner, J. M. (1962). *Growth at Adolescence*. Oxford: Blackwell Scientific Publications.

Tanner, J. M. (1973). Trend towards earlier menarche in London, Oslo, Copenhagen, the Netherlands and Hungary. *Nature*, **243**, 95–96.

Tanner, J. M. and Whitehouse, R. H. (1962). Standards for subcutaneous fat in British children. *British Medical Journal*, *i*, 446–450.

Tanner, J. M. and Whitehouse, R. H. (1975). Revised standards for triceps and subscapular skinfolds in British children. *Archives of Diseases in Childhood*, **50**, 142–145.

Tobias, P. V. (1975). Stature and secular trend among southern African negroes and San (bushmen). *South African Journal of Medical Sciences*, **40**, 145–164.

Aspects of Development
in Contemporary Society

M. P. M. RICHARDS

Medical Psychology Unit, University of Cambridge,
Cambridge, England

Introduction

In the 1930s psychologists and anthropologists of the American culture and personality school attempted to relate specific aspects of child-rearing within a culture to characteristics of the adult society and the patterns and styles of interpersonal relations found in it (e.g. Benedict, 1934; Mead, 1939). The aspects of child-rearing which were singled out for study were largely those that Freudian theory held to be important and included such things as infant feeding, weaning and the control of elimination. With hindsight, I think it is fair to say that the enterprise was not very successful and the links between child-rearing and adult personality that were claimed are not very convincing. The choice of the aspect of child-rearing these studies focused on often seems arbitrary and many other features of the culture that could be explored as potential influences on the development of children were ignored. The influence of this kind of research declined at the time of the Second World War, perhaps because of the taboo on any work which was concerned with national character or simply because most child development research became dominated by questions about individual differences. So at the present time, this research rarely gets a mention in any of the current student texts of developmental psychology.

I want to suggest that this tradition of research did raise important questions even if the methodology it employed left something to be desired. It at least attempted to study development over the life span from childhood to maturity and raised questions about longer-term consequences of early experiences. Though the last decade or so has seen an enormous expansion in research in developmental psychology, the great bulk of this effort has been concerned with describing and analysing processes within childhood rather than exploring longer-term consequences of early events or experiences. So, for instance, most of the research that has grown out of Bowlby's formulations of attachment theory (e.g. Bowlby, 1951; 1969) has been concerned with the nature of parent–infant relationships and their growth, and much less with Bowlby's claims about the life-long consequences of unsatisfactory mother–child attachments for children.

Part of this relative lack of research arises from the obvious difficulties and expense of projects that involve long periods of follow-up and a growing awareness of the methodological weaknesses of the alternative strategy of the retrospective approach. But I think there are at least three reasons why the lack of evidence is unfortunate.

The first is the very widespread belief in our culture that early experience is especially important. Children and infants are seen as much more vulnerable and impressionable than adults. Though it is very difficult to make defensible statements about links between specific early experiences or events and later consequences, few doubt the general proposition that early experience matters (but see Clarke and Clarke, 1976). This leaves parents in a very difficult position. On one hand they are being told, in effect, that what they do with their children is very important because it is likely to have long-term effects. But on the other hand if they enquire about what is most desirable they may well be confronted with conflicting advice and opinion. Fashions among advice-givers tend to change, quickly to add to the general confusion: breast-feeding is essential for a child's future physical and emotional health; feeding method is entirely a matter for a mother to decide on the basis of what she finds convenient and satisfying to her; even a single feed of artificial milk in the first weeks of life can increase the chances of a child suffering from asthma and various allergy conditions; for the first five or six days breast feeds should be carried out every three to four hours and should be limited to a few minutes at each breast; it is very difficult to establish lactation unless very frequent feeds are given for the first week; the baby should be allowed to suck at the breast as long as he likes for the first few days; restricting sucking time early on leads to sore nipples; nipples will be made sore if the baby is allowed to suck for more than four minutes each side; separation of mother and baby at birth, even for a few minutes, creates long-term damage to their relationship; the baby should be removed from the mother at birth for at least several hours while the mother sleeps and recovers.

These are all statements that can be found in the current advice books or that parents report hearing from professional advisers. In some cases we do have research evidence that allows us to make some choice between the alternatives but for others the evidence is inconclusive or just not available.

Clearly it would be desirable to have sufficient evidence available to put advice about child-rearing on a much firmer footing. Not only do we need to know more of the consequences of specific practices but the general belief in the overall importance of early experience deserves more critical attention. Even the most superficial comparison of the ways in which infants are treated in the different cultures of the world suggests that we may over-emphasize the long-term importance of early events. A traveller cannot fail to be impressed by the very wide variety of ways in which infants are cared for and their apparent robustness in the face of practices which many members of our culture would find outrageous.

The second reason why I feel that the lack of research on longer-term consequences is important is that to bring about changes in policies or institutions it seems that evidence of unfavourable long-term consequences is most effective. A good example of this is the change in policies about the visiting by parents of their children when in paediatric wards of hospitals. Until the late 1950s and the rise of the National Association for the Welfare of Children in Hospital, the parental visiting of children in British hospitals was generally very restricted. It was often argued that visits upset children and that the presence of parents would interfere with the smooth running of the ward. What was not in doubt was that children were often very upset while in hospital and cried for their parents and frequently showed behavioural disturbances after they had returned home. Many parents found that the forced separation from their children was very painful. But these obvious and immediate effects on children and parents of admissions were not enough to change visiting policies. Changes only began on any scale when it was argued that the separation brought about by hospital admissions of children could have long-term psychological consequences for the children — a claim, incidentally, which has received some empirical support (e.g. Douglas, 1975). It is now the official policy of the Department of Health and Social Security for paediatric wards to encourage parental visiting and where possible to provide facilities for them to stay overnight. More recently, similar claims about the consequences of early separation (at or around birth) have led to a comparable policy change with regard to special and intensive care baby units.

Though I think most people would agree that the longer some damaging consequence persists, the harder we should strive to remove its cause, I find it strange how little we seem to be concerned with the immediate consequences of some events. Why did many people consider that the frequent distress of children and parents under the old regime of restricted visiting was an insufficient reason to push for change?

My final point concerns the many changes that are occurring in the lives of parents and children. Two that are mentioned elsewhere in this volume are the increasing use of techniques for obstetric "management" and the rising rate of marital separation and divorce. Are these changes that we should welcome or are they causes for concern? How do they influence parents and children? The political system could be used to modify these sorts of changes or to create institutions to cope with their consequences. But sensible political decision-making needs to be informed by accurate evidence of the short- and long-term effects of these changes. How does marital separation influence children? Do the effects vary with the age and sex of the children? Do the custody and access arrangements influence the outcome? What about parental remarriage and step-parenthood? Precise answers to any of these questions are lacking, yet I am discussing a situation which is likely to occur in the lives of about 25% of all children born today. And despite our lack of knowledge, we expect Law Courts and various social welfare agencies to advise parents and even to compel them to follow certain courses of action in the name of "the best interests of the child".

Trends in Research in Developmental Psychology

Earlier I suggested that recent research in developmental psychology had been more concerned with the analysis of processes within infancy and childhood than the long-term consequences of early events and experiences. However, much of this new work seems likely to be very valuable in providing a framework for the investigation of long-term consequences. In this section I want to describe some of the main trends in current research.

Recent work on parent–child relations has stressed the interactive nature of early social encounters. An earlier notion that parental influence is a largely one-way process has been replaced with a model of mutual influence and interdependence of action. This shift has been brought about by the increasing use in human studies of techniques of direct observation originally developed by animal ethologists (see Blurton Jones, 1972) which have provided many examples of interactive processes (e.g. Stern, 1971) and by a growing appreciation of the abilities of babies. Direct observational techniques have most often been applied to the analysis of the behaviour of mothers and babies in feeding or play situations. A simple example from the neonatal period comes from a study I carried out with Judy Dunn (Richards and Bernal, 1972). We were able to show that in early feeding interactions the likelihood of a breastfeeding mother talking to her baby was dependent on whether or not the baby was actually sucking. Sucking does not occur continuously throughout a feed but in short bouts of regularly spaced sucks separated by brief pauses. The mother's talking was most likely to occur in one of these pauses. This example also illustrates the kind of structure and complexity of infant behaviour that has been the subject of much recent research attention. In fact sucking cannot be understood simply as a reaction to outside stimulation but involves autonomous organization by the infant (Richards, 1972). Complexity and surprising sophistication have been repeatedly demonstrated in the investigation of many aspects of infant behaviour and perceptual processes (e.g. Bower, 1979).

The example of the interdependence of a baby's sucking pattern and the timing of the mother's speech can also be used to illustrate how aspects of culture are important even at this detailed level of analysis. If a mother is bottle-feeding the relationship between the baby's sucking and her speech is absent — her talking is as likely to come when the baby is sucking or in a pause. It is probable that the synchrony is lost because the mother is less aware of what the baby is doing — she cannot immediately feel the burst and pauses in the sucking — and she is more likely to be attending to someone else as other people are much more likely to be present during a bottle feed. But my point is that, from the infant's standpoint, the connection between his or her behaviour and that of the mother varied with feeding method. The choice of feeding method is strongly influenced by such things as beliefs about the comparative merits of breast and bottle feeding, the availability of human milk substitutes and attitudes towards sexuality and breasts. So attitudes and beliefs in the culture result in differing inter-active patterns for the infant. Overall, however, the breast and bottle fed babies' experiences do not seem to be so different because what the bottle-fed baby loses in terms of synchronized social inter-change during a feed appears to be made up during other times of his day. Or at least we have no good evidence that differences in feeding method *per se* have important behavioural consequences for development (Richards, 1975).*

Bowlby (1969) regarded the mother–infant relationship as a prototype for later social relationships and as an evolutionary adaptation to reduce the changes of predation for the baby. Later investigators have rather changed this emphasis. They have emphasized the importance of the infant's social interactions as situations which are particularly favourable for the acquisition of language and cognitive skills (e.g. Lock, 1978), correlations have been sought and found between aspects of maternal care and the cognitive and social competence of the infant (e.g. Clarke-Stewart, 1973). With this approach goes a rather different evolutionary argument which sees the lengthening of the period of childhood dependency being closely associated with the development of culture and intelligence. Or in other terms, the growing importance in evolution of our non-genetic modes of intergenerational transfer of information may have created selection pressures for an increased period of childhood dependency. This dependency creates interactive situations which are particularly favourable for the intergenerational transfer of knowledge.

Another area of work which has grown in influence in recent years has been the analysis of motherhood as a social institution and the connections between women's roles as child-rearers and other aspects of their lives (e.g. Rich, 1976; Dinnerstein, 1978; Chodorow, 1978). A constant theme in this analysis is the oppressive nature of child-caring in the isolated home. Research of this kind has originated outside developmental psychology but has helped to turn the attention of psychologists to such problems as depression among the mothers of young children and its effects on the development of children (e.g. Richman, 1976). Not only does this work have practical pay-offs, but it provides a valuable complement to the observational studies I mentioned earlier. Given the nature of observational techniques, it is not surprising that these studies have concentrated on what the psychologist can see rather than what parents may be feeling. This has meant that observational studies have tended to provide a rather cold-blooded picture of social relationships. But work on problems like depression among mothers or parental abuse of children have reminded us of the feelings and emotions of the actors in relationships

---

*It is important to note that other aspects of the feeding method can be very significant for the baby. One of the most important attributes of breast milk is that it can confer resistance to infection on babies. In some situations this can make a very significant difference to their chance of survival.

and the ways in which these are connected to the nature of the social situation and to what passes between parent and child.

The final trend in research I want to mention is the concern with fathers, grandparents, siblings and friends rather than the earlier over-concentration on mothers. A decade ago little writing on the social relations of infants and children mentioned any adult beyond the mother, and the infant's social world was usually conceptualized as a dyad. It is still the case that most child-care is provided by mothers but we have learnt that many other people can be very important for a child. A single dyadic relationship is proving to be too great an over-simplification of the complex social worlds in which children are found. One aspect of this complexity is that children encounter men and women, and their responses to adults are a function of their own gender and that of the adults. This may be seen at a surprisingly early age and is of fundamental importance to understanding gender identity. Gradually our theorizing is beginning to take note of these issues (e.g. Chodorow, 1978). So it is not just that we now find studies on father– as well as mother–child interaction but that developmental-ists are beginning to turn their attention to the dynamics of family relationships and their influence on a child's development (and the influence of the child on the family).

A Contemporary Problem

In this final section of my paper, I want to discuss some aspects of a contemporary problem that seem of special concern to a developmental psychologist. The issue I have selected is the delivery of babies. I chose this partly because it is discussed elsewhere in this volume and I hope that what I have to say may complement what is said there. Other authors have pointed to the very rapid changes that have occurred in obstetric and paediatric techniques. Three aspects of the changes that have occurred over the past couple of generations seem to be particularly likely to influence parent–child relations and I will discuss each in turn.

THE PLACE OF DELIVERY

The place of birth has moved from the familiarity of the home to the unfamilarity of a public institution. The change has been quite rapid with about half of all births occurring at home in the 1940s and now only about two per cent (Davis and Kitzinger, 1978). Interestingly enough, the place of death has shown a very similar tendency. Why should such shifts be significant from the point of view of parent–child relations and the development of children?

No methodologically adequate studies are available which compare home and hospital births so that all we can do is to speculate about the possible consequences of the shift in the place of birth. Effects are likely to be complex because many aspects of the situation are linked to location. For instance, the style of midwifery and obstetrics practised at home may be rather different from that practised in hospital. However, the distinguishing feature of the two situations which I suggest requires most attention is the social context. At home a mother is in a familiar place surrounded by familiar people. Anyone coming to attend a home delivery has to make some concessions to the mother's wishes and is unlikely to be able to "take over" the situation. The tone and style of the social relations that exist among the household members can influence the quality of what goes on between the midwife and/or doctor and the woman. So more often maternity care at home is characterized by qualities such as support and mutual understanding and less likely to be mediated by technical interventions and the kinds of bureaucratic social relations that are typical of large hierarchical institutions. In hospital a labouring woman is a patient and what happens to her is largely a function of physiological processes occurring in her body. At home it is much more difficult for the qualities of a person and the everyday expressions of feelings and wishes which characterize most domestic social interchange to be pushed aside. A mother is surrounded by props and people which serve to maintain the definitions of ordinary daily life. This is all reversed in a hospital where a minimum of props are permitted and the mother's social relations with those from outside the institution are carefully regulated.

Most of us are familiar with institutional social contexts and we are able to behave appropriately in them. The same may be true for the sick or injured when they go to hospital. But when a birth occurs in hospital it becomes a medical event like sickness or injury. I suggest this is important because it could set a mode of interaction for mother and baby. If their social relationship begins in a hospital, it might pick up the bureaucratic, impersonal style. Is it implausible to suggest that the mother might be led to see her baby more in terms of physiology and less as a person? If this is true it could have consequences as several theorists have pointed to the importance of treating infants as if they had the adult attributes of intention and autonomy (Shotter, 1978).

There are no answers to the questions I am raising. We do not know if the social context of the place of delivery influences parent–child relations in the short or long term. All we can be certain of is that the social context is usually very different at home or in a hospital, either from the viewpoint of an observer or from the perspective of a mother (Riley, 1977) and that some parents feel that what happened at the delivery has an important long-term effect on their relations with their child. I might also add that rather similar arguments to mine have been made on the basis of psychoanalytic theory (Lomas, 1978).

The movement towards hospital delivery is, of course, part of much wider changes in our society and, in particular, those related to science, medicine and technology. Medicine has been very important in opening up the very closed Victorian patriarchal family. It has provided a lever for women to use for themselves and their children to counter the power of husbands. At the same time it has opened the family to public control and intervention. For these reasons it would be wrong to put too much emphasis on this one specific social change. However, it is one that is relatively circumscribed, thus making it more amenable to study and, potentially, to further change.

MEDICAL INTERVENTIONS

Modern hospital delivery is characterized by the large number of specific medical interventions that are used to monitor, control or manage physiological functions (Chard and Richards, 1977). These include such things as drugs to control uterine function and pain, devices to monitor the fetal heart rate and surgery to enlarge the vaginal opening. In many cases, where investigations have been carried into possible behavioural effects for the baby, these have been found, though their significance is not always clear. For instance, pain relieving drugs given to the mother pass *via* the placenta to the baby. Among effects that have been demonstrated are a reduction in sucking ability, an increase in sleepiness and reduced social responsiveness. In the long term there have been suggestions of impairment of learning abilities and intelligence (Brackbill, 1979). As far as behavioural development is concerned, there are two kinds of processes that we need to be concerned with. There are those which are the direct result of the drug on the infant's central nervous system. Here it is important to remember that an immature and rapidly growing system may respond quite differently from that of a mature adult. For too many drugs, our knowledge is largely limited to effects on the mature system. The second kind of process is one that has its effects via the interaction of infant and caretaker. A mother is likely to perceive her baby rather differently if he or she spends an unusual amount of time asleep. The eyes are an important signal for social interaction (Robson, 1967). Feeds may become very long drawn out and unsatisfying for the mother if the baby does not suck well. She may feel that the failure is hers as a mother and she is often quite unaware that it could result from the use of a drug during labour (Richards, 1979). Short-term effects of obstetric drugs are well demonstrated (Brackbill, 1979) but we do need to know more about the longer term. Do the changes in interaction that can be seen in the first week or so set up patterns that persist, or do the effects wash out? How far is the image of a baby built up from the initial encounters?

Another point is that the behavioural investigation does not seem able to keep pace with the introduction of new interventions. Often techniques have been in use for several years before good evidence is available about their behavioural effects. Too often assessment is confined to a study of mortality and rather crude measures of morbidity; the more subtle behavioural measures are too rarely used.

POWER

The final characteristic of delivery I want to mention is the relative lack of power that mothers have over the mode of their delivery. The place, manner and even time of delivery are much less often determined by the mother than members of the maternity services. Similarly, in hospital what a mother may do with her baby, and when, is often subject to control by the hospital staff. Not uncommonly a baby is admitted to a Special Care Baby Unit (about 20% of all births) for at least a day or so and this Unit may be in another hospital from where the mother is confined (Brimblecombe et al., 1978). These early separations of mother and baby have been much investigated in recent years and we have evidence that they may influence the parent–child relationship for a period of months if not longer. Typically it is reported that parent–child relations are more distant and less satisfying to the parent after early separation (Richards, 1979). The issue of control appears to be involved in these changes. Parents frequently complain that they did not feel that their child was "theirs" until after discharge from hospital. There are growing suggestions that both in early separation situations and with the use of interventionist obstetric management techniques there are links between the mother's feelings of powerlessness, her later confidence to cope with her baby and her feelings of well-being or depression (Seashore et al., 1973; Oakley, 1980; Kumar and Robson, 1980). Given the surveys that demonstrate high rates of depression among women looking after young children (Brown and Harris, 1978) and the damaging effects of depression on all family members, the possible link between control at delivery and the post-natal period and later well-being and attitudes towards the child are certainly worth a great deal of further investigation. Our society is not one that provides a particularly easy situation for parents, nor does it offer them overmuch in the way of support. For many people, early parenthood is the most stressful part of the life-cycle. We should be very careful that nothing we do increases tensions or reduces self-confidence during this period.

Conclusion

We live in a society which is undergoing continuous and rapid social change. Many of the changes are likely to have far-reaching effects on the lives of parents and children and sometimes on the process of development. However, all too often we only become aware of the ramifying effects of social changes long after the event. I have suggested that we might be wise to take a rather more positive approach towards the assessment and evaluation of change so that decision-making and planning might be better informed.

I have mentioned both short- and long-term effects of events and experiences. Clearly we need to know about both. The self-regulatory processes of development mean that many events may not have long-lasting effects and we must not forget that both consistency and change are common characteristics of development (Dunn, 1979; Brim and Kagan, 1980). Perhaps as a society we are overly concerned about the vulnerability of infants and children to long-term change. However, we have enough examples of seemingly small events which can create profound and long-term effects to make it unwise to confine our attention to the short-term. Amongst the more impressive evidence for long-term effects is that which links the experiences of children to their later performance as parents (e.g. Hall *et al.*, 1979). This makes it particularly important for us to have regard to the more distant future when we consider changes that affect the lives of children.

References

Benedict, R. (1934). *Patterns of Culture*. New York: Houghton Mifflin.

Blurton Jones, N. G. (Editor) (1972). *Ethological Studies of Child Behaviour*. Cambridge: Cambridge University Press.

Bower, T. G. R. (1979). *Human Development*. San Francisco and Reading: W. H. Freeman.

Bowlby, J. (1951). *Maternal Care and Mental Health*. Monograph Series 179. Geneva: World Health Organization.

Bowlby, J. (1969). *Attachment and Loss*. Vol. 1 *Attachment*. London: Hogarth Press.

Brackbill, Y. (1979). Obstetrical medication and infant behavior. In *Handbook of Infant Development*. Edited by J. D. Osofsky. Chichester, Sussex and New York: John Wiley and Sons.

Brimblecombe, F. S. W., Richards, M. P. M. and Roberton, N. R. C. (Editors) (1978). *Early Separation and Special Care Nurseries*. Clinics in Developmental Medicine, No. 68. London: Spastics International Medical Publications/Heinemann Medical Books.

Brim, O. G. and Kagan, J. (Editors) (1980). *Constancy and Change in Human Development*. Cambridge, Massachusetts: Harvard University Press.

Brown, G. W. and Harris, T. (1978). *Social Origins of Depression: A Study of Psychiatric Disorders in Women*. London: Tavistock Publications.

Chard, T. and Richards, M. P. M. (Editors) (1977). *The Benefits and Hazards of the New Obstetrics*. Clinics in Developmental Medicine, No. 64. London: Spastics International Medical Publications/Heinemann Medical Books.

Chodorow, N. (1978). *The Reproduction of Mothering*. Berkeley: University of California Press.

Clarke, A. M. and Clarke, A. D. B. (Editors) (1976). *Early Experience: Myth and Evidence*. London: Open Books.

Clarke-Stewart, K. A. (1973). Interactions between mothers and their young children: characteristics and consequences. *Monographs of the Society for Research in Child Development 38*, No. 153.

Davis, J. and Kitzinger, S. (Editors) (1978). *The Place of Birth*. Oxford: Oxford University Press.

Dinnerstein, D. (1978). *The Rocking of the Cradle, and the Ruling of the World*. London: Souvenir Press.

Douglas, J. W. B. (1975). Early hospital admissions and later disturbances of behaviour and learning. *Developmental Medicine and Child Neurology*, **17**, 456–480.

Dunn, J. (1979). The first year of life: continuities in individual differences. In *The First Year of Life*. Edited by D. Shaffer and J. Dunn. Chichester, Sussex: John Wiley and Sons.

Hall, F., Pawlby, S. J. and Wolkind S. (1979). Early life experiences and later mothering behaviour: a study of mothers and their 20-week-old babies. In *The First Year of Life*. Edited by D. Shaffer and J. Dunn. Chichester, Sussex: John Wiley and Sons.

Kumar, R. and Robson, K. (1980). *Delayed Onset of Maternal Affection After Childbirth*. Unpublished paper. London: Institute of Psychiatry.

Lock, A. (Editor) (1978). *Action, Gesture and Symbol: The Emergence of Language*. London: Academic Press.

Lomas, P. (1978). An interpretation of modern obstetric practice. In *The Place of Birth*. Edited by J. Davis and S. Kitzinger. Oxford: Oxford University Press.

Mead, M. (1939). *Sex and Temperament in Three Primitive Societies*. New York: William Morrow.

Oakley, A. (1980). *Women Confined: Towards a Sociology of Childbirth*. Oxford: Martin Robinson.

Rich, A. (1976). *Of Women Born: Motherhood as Experience and Institution.* New York: W. W. Norton.

Richards, M. P. M. (1972). Social interaction in the first weeks of human life. *Psychiatrica, Neurologica and Neurochirica,* **74**, 35–47.

Richards, M. P. M. (1975). Feeding and the early growth of the mother–child relationship. In *Modern Problems in Pediatrics No. 15.* Edited by N. Kretchmer, E. Rossi and F. Sereni. Basel: Karger.

Richards, M. P. M. (1979). Effects on development of medical interventions and the separation of newborns from their parents. In *The First Year of Life.* Edited by D. Schaffer and J. Dunn. Chichester, Sussex: John Wiley and Sons.

Richards, M. P. M. and Bernal, J. F. (1972). An observational study of mother–infant interaction. In *Ethological Studies of Child Behavior.* Edited by N. G. Blurton Jones. Cambridge: Cambridge University Press.

Richman, N. (1976). Depression in mothers of pre-school children. *Journal of Child Psychology and Psychiatry,* **17**, 75–78.

Riley, E. M. D. (1977). 'What do women want?' — the question of choice in the conduct of labour. In *The Benefits and Hazards of the New Obstetrics.* Edited by T. Chard and M. P. M. Richards. Clinics in Developmental Medicine, No. 64. London: Spastics International Medical Publications/Heinemann Medical Books.

Robson, K. S. (1967). The role of eye-to-eye contact in maternal–infant attachment. *Journal of Child Psychology and Psychiatry,* **8**, 13–25.

Seashore, M. J., Leifer, A. D., Barnett, C. R. and Leiderman, P. H. (1973). The effects of denial of early mother–infant interaction on maternal self-confidence. *Journal of Personality and Social Psychology,* **3**, 369–378.

Shotter, J. (1978). The cultural context of communication studies: theoretical and methodological issues. In *Action, Gesture and Symbol: The Emergence of Language.* Edited by A. Lock. London: Academic Press.

Stern, D. N. (1971). A micro-analysis of mother–infant interaction. *Journal of American Academy of Child Psychiatry,* **10**, 501–517.

Generational Continuities
in Child-Rearing Practices

ALEX McGLAUGHLIN*

*Department of Social Administration, University of Hull,
Hull, England*

The commonly held belief that child-rearing refers to a set of specifiable and agreed behaviours simply is not true. Historically, interpretations have varied from the simple act of lifting, or "raising", the newborn infant from the ground, in recognition of paternity, to the nurturance and encouragement of all aspects of physical, social, emotional and cognitive development, from birth through to maturity. In this century, the features of child-rearing on which research has successively focused (and in the main with which parents have been most concerned) have been influenced as much by social change and fashion as by theory and knowledge. The emphasis has moved from simple physical care to exploration of care-giver beliefs and attitudes, then to increased stimulation and currently to complex interaction. In 1903 the probability of not surviving beyond the fifteenth year was one in five. By 1933 this had fallen to one in eleven and is now less than one in fifty (Miller, 1973). Indeed, the age range one to fifteen years is now associated with low mortality (see W. A. Marshall, this volume). This largely medical success was in part responsible for the shift of interest away from basic care-giving and towards the attitudes of the mother in care-giving. The concurrent influence of Freudian theory needs little elaboration: the hypothesizing of oral, anal and phallic stages of development led to research on feeding, toilet, sex and aggression training practices (e.g. Whiting and Child, 1953; Sears *et al.*, 1957). Despite the growing emancipation of women, especially during the 1940s, the World Health Organization monograph authored by Bowlby (1951) helped to ensure continued concentration on aspects of the mother–child dyad and renewal of the search for single-factor

*The assistance of Dr. Janet Empson, Dr. Jill Sever and Maura Morrissey is gratefully acknowledged.

explanations of differences in children's development, especially personality. Bowlby's own recantation and reformulation of the earlier hypotheses, just a few years later, was virtually ignored (Bowlby et al., 1956). In the event, the search failed and a further paradigm shift occurred. Stimulation and cognitive gain became the major focus of attention, as exemplified by papers such as "Cognitive Elements in Maternal Behaviour" (Hess and Shipman, 1967). The shift was relatively swift and, at least in America, rapidly followed by action, in the form of Project Headstart. But although the focus of interest had changed, the approach was still embedded in deficit theory. The notion remained that somehow, something had to be "put into" the child. This simple and mistaken conceptualization persisted because the unidirectional model of behaviour had been retained. Recognition had not yet been given to the powerful effects that infants may have on their care-givers (Stolz, 1967; Bell, 1968; Lewis and Rosenblum, 1974; Bell and Harper, 1977; Lerner and Spanier, 1978) or to the importance of people other than the primary care-giver (e.g. Rapoport et al., 1977; Parke, 1979; Mueller and Vandell, 1979). The lack of balance led one author, having examined child-rearing manuals in America between 1913 and 1976, to the conclusion that such manuals should be viewed as "mother-rearing tracts which have as much to say about the lives of women as about the children for whom they are caring" (Weiss, 1978). Thus it is now becoming an increasingly accepted view that child-rearing and development need to be considered in a far broader context than is provided by the mother–child dyad alone.

The foregoing analysis is not novel. Other authors have noted a similar pattern of change (Dreitzel, 1973; Newson and Newson, 1974; Wood, 1977). But a historical perspective is necessary in order to address the question of whether there are any generational continuities in child-rearing. For as the focus of interest has changed over time, so too has the type of data collected. In consequence, both the main comparative approaches are unsatisfactory. That is, if we collect current data on practices examined in the past, such practices are unlikely to be of any real interest now. Alternatively, if we look at practices which are of current interest, we have little or no previous data for comparison. In addition, although most studies of child-rearing have been concerned with the earliest years of childhood, many have concentrated on one narrow age range within this period, which may vary between one investigation and another. The possibility that different skills may be important at different child ages, and that the parenting experience may itself affect parental attitudes and behaviours, has also largely been ignored (Maccoby, 1980). Indeed, recent concern with the methodology of developmental research and the basic requirements of an acceptable study (Yarrow *et al.*, 1968; Wohlwill, 1973; Nesselroade and Baltes, 1979) casts serious doubt on the approach and findings of many of the available studies. Finally, if our interest is in studies of child-rearing practices across generations of the same families, there are exceedingly few of them; and none at all employing a complex interactional paradigm.

In the remainder of this paper, therefore, we shall draw upon a variety of data sources, and particularly our own work with sixty disadvantaged families in Humberside, over the past five years (McGlaughlin, 1980).* It is important to note that our families were recruited to the study in pairs. The mothers in each pair are sisters (siblings), each of whom either had a child under one year of age or was pregnant at the start of the study. Thus we can estimate the extent of similarity in child-rearing practices that exists between members of the same family generation, i.e. intra-generational similarity.

We shall argue that change is the more general rule, even though some measure of continuity can be demonstrated, and that this is the case whether we compare: (i) different families across time and place; (ii) different generations of the same families; or (iii) different members of both the same generation and family, i.e. sibling mothers. The coverage is selective and illustrative rather than exhaustive.

First, what can we learn from the literature? The general picture of disagreement which emerges is perhaps put most directly in a recent wide-ranging review of child-care in Britain. Pringle and Naidoo (1974) state:

> "there are few explicitly stated concepts about children or principles of child-rearing which would be agreed to by most people in this country" (page 11).

Similarly, Rutter and Madge (1976) conclude:

> "Patterns of parenting in the population as a whole show marked shifts" (page 224),

while Robinson *et al.* (1973), commenting on child-rearing in America, state:

> "there is no agreed-upon way to bring up children" (page 11).

---

*In the tables which follow N is sometimes less than 60. Questions could not always be answered or observations completed, e.g. where the child was in care.

Even expert opinion appears to be highly unstable. Benjamin Spock wrote a monthly column for parents, in the *Ladies Home Journal*, over a ten-year period, starting in the mid-1950s. The type of advice given in this column during the first and last eighteen months of publication, has been analysed (unpublished) and referred to in Robinson *et al.* (1973). The considerable change in the various types of advice given, as between the mid-1950s and the mid-1960s, is illustrated in Table I. Emphasis on nurturance and permissiveness decreased, while advice to discipline, judged by recommendations to set rules and limits or

Table I

The changed pattern in the advice given by one expert on child-rearing: a comparison of two periods

Advice	Period of Analysis	
	Mid 1950s	Mid 1960s
	%	%
1. Nurturance	22	2
2. Permissiveness	29	10
3. Setting Rules and Limits	6	12
4. Redirecting Child Behaviour	1	10
5. Cognitive Experience	1	9
6. Other	41	57

redirect the child's behaviour, increased, as also did recommendations for increased cognitive experience. We know that there is "some correspondence between recommended values and practices, and those subsequently espoused by parents" (Kohn, 1969, page 379). But it is not clear whether parents are directly influenced by professional opinion, or both are changing as a result of overall change within the culture. In either case, however, change rather than stability appears to be the outcome.

Given this background of historical shift, lack of agreement within cultures as to principles of child-rearing, and changes in professional advice, it is hardly surprising that continuities are difficult to find. Yet there are some interesting trends. Two features of child-rearing which illustrate this are breastfeeding and father participation. The former is a practice of longstanding interest, whereas the latter has gained prominence only in more recent years. A comparison of the findings on breastfeeding in four surveys is given in Table II. As can be seen, there is a marked trend away from breastfeeding. In the Humberside

Table II
Proportion of mothers still breastfeeding at various ages: surveys compared

	1 month %	3 months %	6 months %
Newcastle (1947–8)	78	42	31
Bristol (1947–8)	67	44	32
Nottingham (1959–60)	54	29	13
Humberside (1975–76) (working class only)	18	10	3

sample, only 18 percent of our 60 mothers were breastfeeding their infants by one month of age, and just three percent at six months. Of course, each of the surveys refers to a different geographical region and both sample size and class composition vary. In addition, since 1975 there has been considerable pressure exerted by the medical and allied professions to encourage breastfeeding. It would be unwise therefore simply to assume that the trend noted has continued during subsequent years.

Father participation in child-rearing is considered in Table III. The Nottingham results are fully reported by Newson and Newson (1963). The Humberside findings are based on our smaller sample of 60 families and on the same questions as were asked in Nottingham. With the exception of the question asking if father ever took the child out without mother, the Humberside fathers are more participative in every area assessed. This lends support to the argument that fathers are becoming increasingly involved in child-rearing. The fact that the Humberside fathers are less likely to take their child out alone could even be consonant with this view. That is to say, this finding might simply be the corollary of an increase in outings involving the whole family, or of an increasing willingness on the part of fathers to become involved in child-rearing activities within the home (leaving less time for solo outings). Equally likely, however, are explanations in terms of stereotyping and cultural differences. Thus it may be that increased father participation is occurring only for those aspects of child-rearing which take place within the home, with its relative privacy. Or perhaps, for Humberside fathers, there are community pressures against solo outings which are more severe than those to be found in Nottingham. Our impression is that the latter explanation is the most likely. Overall, the trend is encouraging, but it would be wrong to use these data as a basis for inferring the general level of involvement of

Table III
Percentage of fathers undertaking various activities in the care of one-year-olds

Frequency		Play with	Feed him	Take Out Alone	Change Nappy	Attend in Night	Bath him
Often	Humberside 1975/76	92	37	14	25	25	19
	Nottingham 1959/60	83	34	29	20	18	15
Sometimes	Humberside 1975/76	7	43	41	41	29	25
	Nottingham 1959/60	16	44	39	37	32	24
Never	Humberside 1975/76	1	20	45	34	46	56
	Nottingham 1959/60	1	22	32	43	50	61

fathers in the rearing of their infants. Newson and Newson (1963) conclude from their survey: "the head of the household chooses to sit at his own fireside, a baby on his knee and a feeding bottle in his hand: the modern father's place is in the home" (page 147). Richards *et al.* (1977), referring to their own follow-up study on father participation, state: "Our results, like those of the Newsons (1963) in Nottingham, show that only a minority of fathers take a regular part in looking after their children" (page 33). The interpretation rests on whether the greatest impression is created by the proportion of fathers who often participate in child-rearing, or those who never do so, tempered by consideration as to the overall importance of the few activities appearing in Table III.

Some interesting, if less direct, evidence of the shift towards greater father participation, is provided by Barnes (1980). When over two hundred of the boys from the Newson's Nottingham sample were interviewed at the age of sixteen their *intended* level of early father participation was higher than the actual level of their fathers in the late 1950s and also of the Humberside sample. Direct comparisons between the Nottingham fathers' actions and their sons' intentions should provide valuable information on the degree of continuity between the two generations.

Indeed, the major obstacle to informed debate of the inter-generational continuities issue is the scarcity of hard evidence. "Despite the widespread belief that how parents were themselves brought up will influence how they treat their own children, there is only one study of this'' (Rutter and Madge, 1976, page 232). The one study (Frommer and O'Shea, 1973a, b) found that it was current marital problems, rather than the parents' own childhood experiences, which were most strongly associated with difficulties in infant management. A less satisfactory restrospective study (Bronson *et al.*, 1959) concluded that ''on the whole people do *not* follow the example of their parents'', and this view receives some support from our own findings. Our 60 mothers were asked whether or not they felt they were bringing up their child in the same way as they had been reared. The replies are summarized in Table IV.

Table IV
Mothers intending to bring up their child as they were reared (N = 58) Humberside sample

(a)	Individual mothers who are so intending	22	
	Individual mothers who are not intending to do so	36	
(b)	Numbers of *pairs* of mothers (sisters) who both say they are	4	
	Number of pairs of mothers (sisters) who both say they are not	11	} 15 similar pairs
	Sister pairs disagreed	14	

Rather more of our mothers (36) said their own upbringing and their child's were different, than said they were similar (22). Fifteen pairs of mothers (siblings) gave the same answer to this question, whereas 14 pairs gave opposite answers. However, of the 15 pairs of siblings who gave the same answer, the clear majority (11 pairs) were agreed in raising their children differently from their own upbringing. Thus the tendency is for the next generation to choose to rear differently; a movement towards change which is concentrated within particular families. However, the differences are neither marked, nor particularly reliable (Chi^2 = 3.39, d.f. = 1, p < 0.10), and may not be true of other populations. The fact that our sample is a disadvantaged one may have implications for the ways in which our mothers were reared and their reactions to that upbringing in raising their own children. We have some evidence to support this latter suggestion. Each mother was asked to tell us where she looked for advice on problems with her child. In 52 of our families the child's maternal grandmother was alive and living locally. Mothers in 37 of these families sought advice from the maternal grandmother (see Table V).

Table V
Reference to maternal grandmother for advice on child-rearing difficulties (N = 52)
Humberside sample

(a)	Individual mothers who do seek advice from Granny	37	
	Individual mothers who do not seek advice from Granny	15	
(b)	Number of pairs of mothers (sisters) who both seek advice from Granny	14	} 17 similar pairs
	Number of pairs of mothers (sisters) who do not seek advice from Granny	3	
	Sister pairs disagreed (one does the other does not seek Granny's advice)	9	

Six mothers never sought advice, whilst friends, relatives, a sister, the clinic, husband, health visitor and general practitioner were each consulted by between nine and fourteen of our mothers. Thus the maternal grandmother is clearly a major source of advice on child-rearing. However, within this group, 32 mothers told us that they were not rearing their child as they were raised, and of these, approaching half (13) said they did *not* seek advice from Granny. In contrast, 20 mothers in this group told us that they were rearing their child as they were raised, but only three said they did *not* seek advice from Granny. This in part explains the paradox posed by the answers to these two questions; that is, a majority of our mothers claim not to be raising their child as they were raised, yet a further majority say they look to their child's grandmother for advice. However, the finding might not be characteristic of other samples (Chi^2 = 3.79, d.f. = 1, $p < 0.10$). Table V also shows how far our sibling mothers are alike in seeking advice from their mother. Only nine of our 26 pairs of mothers are unalike in this respect, i.e. one does seek her mother's advice whilst the other does not. Of the other 17 pairs, in 14 both seek their mother's advice, whereas in only three pairs does neither sister look to mother for advice. This familial similarity of our sibling mothers is quite strong and particularly so where Granny is considered to be a source of advice (Chi^2 = 5.97, d.f. = 1, $p < 0.025$).

An aspect of child-rearing practice which is receiving increasing attention is that of discipline, punishment and, more particularly, physical abuse. Abnormal parenting has been identified as the single most likely pattern to be directly reproduced in the next generation. Thus parents who themselves experienced aggression in childhood are more likely to become violent parents (Gelles, 1972; Scott, 1973) and some authors have traced battering through several generations of the same families (e.g. Oliver and Taylor, 1971; Oliver and Cox, 1973). The relevant information from our study is the use of smacking by mothers, in disciplining their one-year-old infants. It can be seen in Table VI that the majority of our mothers do find it necessary to use smacking, although a substantial number never do (43:17). Compared

Table VI
Attitude towards smacking one-year old child (n = 60) Humberside sample

(a)	Individual mothers who consider it is necessary to smack	43	
	Individual mothers who consider it is not necessary to smack	17	
(b)	Number of *pairs* of mothers (sisters) who consider it is necessary to smack	16	} 19 similar pairs
	Number of *pairs* of mothers (sisters) who consider it is not necessary to smack	3	
	Sister pairs disagreed (one considers smacking necessary the other does not)	11	

with the findings in Nottingham (Newson and Newson, 1963) this suggests that rather more of our mothers are smacking their one-year-old children, even when class composition is taken into account. If this indicates a trend towards increased use of physical methods of discipline, it is decidedly disturbing. The public, and sometimes professional, confusion of discipline with physical punishment has often led to erroneous debate and an unfortunate neglect of the compelling evidence that physical punishment is a counter-productive method of discipline (British Psychological Society, 1980; Maccoby, 1980; Herbert, 1978; Hersov and Berger, 1978). It can also be seen from Table VI that our sibling mothers are more likely than not to behave alike in their use of smacking. Thus of the 30 pairs of sisters, in only 11 pairs does one resort to smacking whilst the other does not. Further, in 16 of the 19 pairs who behave alike over smacking, both do use smacking. This suggests that there is a familial influence, fostering recourse to smacking as a means of discipline. This association is both strong and highly significant statistically ($Chi^2 = 8.15$, d.f. $= 1$, p $<$

0.01). We cannot say as yet whether this familial similarity is more likely to be the result of the shared earlier experience of the sibling mothers; the contemporary influence of one sister on the other, or of their mother on both; or of some other factor.

The discussion so far has been based on data primarily derived from interviews and self-report. Considerable evidence on child-rearing and child development has now accumulated through direct observation (e.g. Clarke-Stewart, 1973; White and Watts, 1973; White, 1978; White et al., 1979; Lewis and Rosenblum, 1977; Schaffer, 1977; Schaffer and Dunn, 1979). A major part of our own work has been the collection and analysis of videotape recorded (VTR) observations of our mothers and their children, playing and eating together in their own homes. I shall conclude this section with a consideration of some of these data: first demonstrating the link between what we have observed mothers and children doing together and the later measured language performance of their children; and secondly, considering the degree to which sibling mothers can be observed to behave similarly with their children. The data base is a nine-minute recording of each of our 60 mothers and children playing together, repeated when each child was 12, 18, 24 and 30 months of age. Each nine-minute sequence was divided into 30 units of 18 seconds. For each such unit we determined whether an interaction had occurred, its type (e.g. social or intellectual), the initiator (mother, child, other) and the technique employed by mother (e.g. facilitating, directing, teaching etc). We also noted the use of speech to the child, the responsiveness of the child and a number of other features of interaction. Full details, together with comments on observer reliability and stability of the observed behaviours over time, can be found in McGlaughlin (1980) and McGlaughlin et al. (1980). Four behaviours only will be considered here, chosen because they show the greatest consistency both at and across each of the four child ages observed. The four are:

i. *Total Interactions:* a simple count of the total number of eighteen-second observation units in which an interaction took place (maximum possible, 30).

ii. *Intellectual type:* a simple count of the number of interactions [i above] which were of an intellectual type, i.e. focused on cognitive growth, e.g. naming, labelling, demonstrating, functions of things.

iii. *Teaching:* a simple count of the number of interactions [i above] in which mother's main technique was to teach.

iv. *Speech to Child:* a simple count of the number of interactions [i above] in which mother used speech to her child.

At 30 months of age each child was assessed on the Reynell Development Language Scales (Reynell, 1969). The correlations between each of the four behavioural measures at each child age, and performance on the Reynell at 30 months, are shown in Fig. 1.

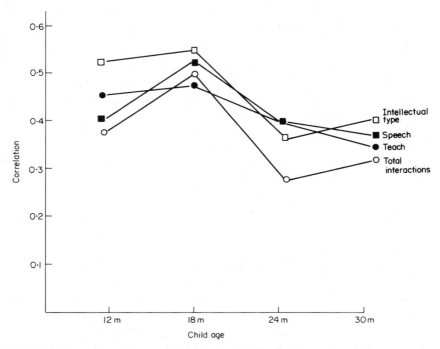

FIG. 1. Correlations between observed mother–child interactions at four child ages, and language scores at 30 months. (N = 60).

All these correlations are statistically significant and vary between 0.3 and 0.55. As noted earlier, it is unlikely that there is a strong single factor explanation for differences in children's development and performance. We would not therefore expect any one of these behavioural measures to account for all the variance on our measure of language performance. However we should expect them, when taken in combination together with wider environmental measures (e.g. of stress from life events and circumstances), to account for an increasing proportion of that variance. This is in fact the case (McGlaughlin *et al.*, 1981); a point we shall discuss later. But the main concern of this chapter is generational continuities. To address this issue directly, we have compared the variation within each of our pairs of sibling mothers with the variation between the thirty pairs. The procedure chosen for this comparison is often used in twin studies and treats each pair of sisters as a class, with n = 2. If each pair of sisters is identical, yet different from every other pair, then the intraclass correlation will equal plus one. If the mean values of each class (pair of sisters) are identical, then all the variance will be within the classes and the correlation will equal minus one. Thus *intra-generational continuity* is suggested by positive correlations and *discontinuity* by negative correlations. Figure 2 plots the intra-class correlations, at each child age, for the four variables of observed mother–child interaction discussed above. Clearly, sibship is a variable of some importance; none of the correlations are below zero, whilst the largest is above plus 0.6 (teaching at 30 months child age).

It would also appear that on the four selected aspects of mother–child behaviour, sibling mothers show increasing similarity as their children grow older. The greatest level of similarity occurs at 30 months child age and the least at 18 months. Unfortunately, we do not as yet have any information on the families at later ages. The importance of these intra-class correlations is debatable. Compared against the size of correlation reported for twins on both physical and psychological measures (Kamin, 1974; Fischbein, 1977), they are not impressive. But they do approach the level of correlation between siblings on measures of intelligence (Maxwell, 1961).

Viewed in an intergenerational perspective, they clearly would not encourage us to expect much similarity between generations, since there is so little similarity within a generation. But this is far too simple a conclusion if we are to take the complex-interaction model seriously. Other data in our study indicate that stress factors, concerned with health, employment, housing and finance, are associated with the same dependent measure of child development and may operate through their effect on the mother–child relationship, i.e. by suppressing, amplifying or otherwise distorting interaction (Empson and McGlaughlin, 1979). We also know that our sibling mothers show very little correspondence in the levels of stress to which they are subjected. Given these differences, and the varied characteristics of the infants themselves, so far unconsidered, it is perhaps surprising that our sibling mothers show any degree of similarity at all. It may be that once we take account of the children's own characteristics and of the wider contextual differences, our sibling mothers will demonstrate a remarkable level of similarity in their behaviour. We expect to complete such an analysis and to report the findings in the future.

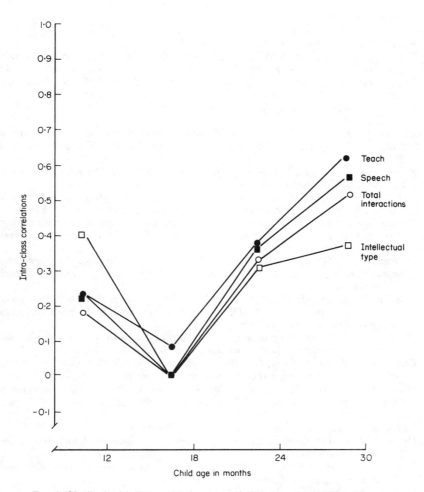

FIG. 2. Similarity in observed behaviour of sibling mother. (N = 60).

Acknowledgement

The work reported herein was in part supported by the financial assistance of the Joint DHSS/SSRC Working Party on Transmitted Deprivation and the SSRC Grant HR5017/1.

References

Barnes, P. (1980). Personal Communication.

Bell, R. Q. (1968). A reinterpretation of the direction of effects in studies of socialization. *Psychological Review*, **75**, 81–95.

Bell, R. Q. and Harper, L. V. (1977). *Child Effects on Adults*. Hillsdale, New Jersey: Lawrence Erlbaum Associates.

Bowlby, J. (1951). *Maternal Care and Mental Health*. Monograph Series 179. Geneva: World Health Organization.

Bowlby, J., Ainsworth, M., Boston, M. and Rosenbluth, D. (1956). The effects of mother–child separation: a follow-up study. *British Journal of Medical Psychology*, **29**, 211–247.

British Psychological Society (1980). *Corporal Punishment in Schools*. Working Party Report. Leicester: British Psychological Society.

Bronson, W. C., Katten, E. S. and Livson, N. (1959). Patterns of authority and affection in two generations. *Journal of Abnormal and Social Psychology*, **58**, 143–152.

Clarke-Stewart, K. A. (1973). Interactions between mothers and their young children: characteristics and consequences. *Monographs of the Society for Research in Child Development*, **38**, (6–7).

Dreitzel, H. P. (1973). Introduction: childhood and socialization. In *Childhood and Socialization*. Edited by H. P. Dreitzel. New York and London: Macmillan Publishers.

Empson, J. M. and McGlaughlin, A. (1979). *Stress Factors in the Lives of Disadvantaged Children*. Paper presented to the Developmental Section of the British Psychological Society Annual Conference, Nottingham, April 1977.

Fischbein, S. (1977). Intra-pair similarity in physical growth of monozygotic and of dizygotic twins during puberty. *Annals of Human Biology*, **4**, 417–430.

Frommer, E. A. and O'Shea, G. (1973a). Antenatal identification of women liable to have problems in managing their infants. *British Journal of Psychiatry*, **123**, 149–156.

Frommer, E. A. and O'Shea, G. (1973b). The importance of childhood experience in relation to problems of marriage and family-building. *British Journal of Psychiatry*, **123**, 157–160.

Gelles, R. J. (1972). *The Violent Home*. Beverley Hills: Sage.

Herbert, M. (1978). *Conduct Disorders of Childhood and Adolescence*. Chichester, Sussex: John Wiley and Sons.

Hersov, L. A. and Berger, M. (Editors) (1978). *Aggression and Antisocial Behaviour in Childhood and Adolescence*. Oxford: Pergamon Press.

Hess, R. D. and Shipman, V. C. (1967). Cognitive elements in maternal behavior. In *Minnesota Symposia on Child Psychology*. Volume 1, edited by J. P. Hill. Minneapolis: University of Minnesota Press.

Kamin, L. J. (1974). *The Science and Politics of I.Q.* Hillsdale, New Jersey: Lawrence Erlbaum Associates.

Kohn, M. L. (1969). *Class and Conformity: A Study of Values*. Homewood, Illinois. The Dorsey Press.

Lerner, R. M. and Spanier, G. B. (Editors) (1978). *Child Influences on Marital and Family Interaction: A Life-Span Perspective*. London: Academic Press.

Lewis, M. and Rosenblum, L. A. (Editors) (1974). *The Effect of the Infant on its Caregiver*. Chichester, Sussex: John Wiley and Sons.

Lewis, M. and Rosenblum, L. A. (Editors) (1977). *Interaction, Conversation, and the Development of Language*. Chichester, Sussex: John Wiley and Sons.

Maccoby, E. E. (1980). *Social Development: Psychological Growth and the Parent–Child Relationship.* New York and London: Harcourt Brace Jovanovich.

McGlaughlin, A. (1980). *Early Child Development and the Home Environment.* End of Grant Report to the Social Science Research Council, HR 5017/1.

McGlaughlin, A., Empson, J. M., Morrissey, M. and Sever, J. (1980). Early child development and the home environment: consistencies at and between four pre-school stages. *International Journal of Behavioural Development*, **3**, 299–309.

McGlaughlin, A., Morrissey, M., Empson, J. M. and Sever, J. (1981). Language performance at 30 months in a sample of disadvantaged children: interpersonal and environmental influences. In *Communication in Child Development.* Edited by W. P. Robinson. London: Academic Press.

Maxwell, J. (1961). *The Level and Trend of National Intelligence.* London: Hodder and Stoughton Educational.

Miller, F. J. W. (1973). Social paediatrics. In *Textbook of Paediatrics.* Edited by J. O. Forfar and G. C. Arneil. Edinburgh: Churchill Livingstone.

Mueller, E. C. and Vandell, D. (1979). Infant–infant interaction. In *Handbook of Infant Development.* Edited by J. D. Osofsky. Chichester, Sussex: John Wiley and Sons.

Nesselroade, J. R. and Baltes, P. B. (Editors) (1979). *Longitudinal Research in the Study of Behaviour and Development.* London: Academic Press.

Newson, J. and Newson, E. (1963). *Infant Care in an Urban Community.* London: George Allen and Unwin.

Newson, J. and Newson, E. (1974). Cultural aspects of child-rearing in the English-speaking world. In *The Integration of a Child into a Social World.* Edited by M. P. M. Richards. Cambridge: Cambridge University Press.

Oliver, J. E. and Cox, J. (1973). A family kindred with ill-used children: the burden on the community. *British Journal of Psychiatry*, **123**, 81–90.

Oliver, J. E. and Taylor, A. (1971). Five generations of ill-treated children in one family pedigree. *British Journal of Psychiatry*, **119**, 473–480.

Parke, R. D. (1979). Perspectives on father–infant interaction. In *Handbook of Infant Development.* Edited by J. D. Osofsky. Chichester, Sussex: John Wiley and Sons.

Pringle, M. L. K. and Naidoo, S. (1974). Early child care in Britain. *Early Child Development and Care*, **3** (4). Special Monograph Issue.

Rapoport, R., Rapoport, R. N. and Strelitz, Z. (1977). *Fathers, Mothers and Others: Towards New Alliances.* London: Routledge and Kegan Paul.

Reynell, J. (1969). *Reynell Developmental Language Scales.* Slough: National Foundation for Educational Research.

Richards, M. P. M., Dunn, J. F. and Antonis, B. (1977). Caretaking in the first year of life: the role of fathers, and mothers' social isolation. *Child: Care, Health and Development*, **3**, 23–36.

Robinson, H. B., Robinson, N. M., Wolins, M., Bronfenbrenner, U. and Richmond, J. B. (1973). Early child care in the United States of America. *Early Child Development and Care*, **2** (4). Special Monograph Issue.

Rutter, M. and Madge, N. (1976). *Cycles of Disadvantage.* London: Heinemann.

Schaffer, H. R. (Editor) (1977). *Studies in Mother–Infant Interaction.* London: Academic Press.

Schaffer, H. R. and Dunn, J. (Editors) (1979). *The First Year of Life.* Chichester, Sussex: John Wiley and Sons.

Scott, P. D. (1973). Fatal battered baby cases. *Medicine, Science and the Law*, **13**, 197–206.

Sears, R., Maccoby, E. E. and Levin, H. (1957). *Patterns of Childrearing.* Evanston, Illinois: Row, Peterson and Co.

Stolz, L. M. (1967). *Influences on Parent Behaviour*. London: Tavistock Publications.

Weiss, N. P. (1978). The mother–child dyad revisited: perceptions of mothers and children in twentieth-century child rearing manuals. *Journal of Social Issues*, **34**, 29–45.

White, B. L. (1978). *Experience and Environment*, Vol. II Englewood Cliffs, New Jersey: Prentice Hall.

White, B. L. and Watts, J. C. (1973). *Experience and Environment*, Vol. I. Englewood Cliffs, New Jersey: Prentice Hall.

White, B. L., Kaban, B. T. and Attanucci, J. S. (1979). *The Origins of Human Competence*. Lexington, Massachusetts: D. C. Heath.

Whiting, J. W. M. and Child, I. L. (1953). *Child Training and Personality: Cross-Cultural Study*. New Haven: Yale University Press.

Wohlwill, J. F. (1973). *The Study of Behavioral Development in Children*. New York and London: Academic Press.

Wood, M. E. (1977). Changing social attitudes to childhood. In *Equalities and Inequalities in Family Life*. Edited by R. Chester and J. Peel. Proceedings of the Thirteenth Annual Symposium of the Eugenics Society. London: Academic Press.

Yarrow, M. R., Campbell, J. D. and Burton, R. V. (1968). *Child Rearing: An Enquiry into Research and Methods*. San Francisco: Jossey-Bass Publishers.

Contemporary Child-Rearing in Evolutionary Perspective

N. G. BLURTON JONES

Department of Growth and Development,
Institute of Child Health, London, England

Introduction

There are several ways in which an "evolutionary perspective" may help us to understand or see with fresh eyes the way we rear our children. Each of these must be approached with caution for however well argued, evolution provides perspectives, not data nor proofs about effects of child-rearing. The subject is large, and two of the areas are growing rapidly but I shall attempt to outline several aspects of the subject.

First I will deal briefly with the comparison of contemporary child-rearing with child-rearing in man's pre-history. Two questions must be kept separate: (1) what can we establish about prehistoric child-rearing? (2) if there are differences between now and then, do they matter for children or parents, is there justification for the romantic back-to-nature viewpoint?

Second, I will outline approaches in which the infant, its development and care are thought of as the products of evolution. Recent developments of evolutionary theory have yet to make their mark on ideas or direct research on socialization but probably will in the future (e.g. Harpending, 1980), for better or worse. The definition of inclusive fitness by Hamilton (1964), and the development of studies of animal behaviour as optimizing systems, maximizing an individual's inclusive fitness, and theoretical derivations from inclusive fitness such as parent–offspring conflict theory (Trivers, 1974; Parker and Macnair, 1979) require a rethinking of the study of population regulation and may lead evolutionary theorists eventually to make interesting and testable predictions about socialization and interaction within families. But I will deal at greater length with a so far much more constant and productive perspective that originated partly from an evolutionary perspective: the child is not a passive recipient of socialization, it arrives able to provoke interaction and continues thus, shaping the environment in which it develops.

Prehistoric Child Rearing Practices

There are not and never will be any direct data on prehistoric child-rearing patterns. But this behaviour need not remain as a permanent projective test for theories in child development. There are four lines of enquiry that provide evidence about some aspects of child raising in our prehistory. If two or more of these independent lines give similar conclusions we may feel some confidence in these conclusions.

ARCHAEOLOGY

Archaeological techniques advance endlessly and it would be foolish to suppose that the present shortage of even circumstantial evidence about child raising in preagricultural man will continue. Many kinds of information could be of use. I am not an archaeologist and do not know all the data one could use. But even data such as proportion of children in a population cannot be established, only a group instantly killed by some catastrophe could give us any indication. The odd child skeleton does exist but gives us no indication of the numbers of babies dying, though cause of death may be deduced. There is evidence of death or injury to children by predators. Some children's footprints, and children's handprints on rock or cave paintings have been found. These show that children were not excluded from these important, supposedly sacred places. Settlement patterns, indicated by hearths, stones and bones can be informative. They tend towards confirming the impression from contemporary hunter–gatherers that bands of 25–40 people were common, almost standard. Useful but steadily dating reference books are Washburn (1961), Lee and DeVore (1968), Pfeiffer (1974).

CROSS-CULTURAL CONSTANTS

There is an argument, not one I would want to push too hard, that if there are features of human behaviour present in all cultures, they are characteristic of our species, evolved, and perhaps rather environment-resistant. Of course it is conceivable that they are present because all people go through certain identical learning processes. But if a feature is present in all of the several hundred cultures studied, the chances of its being absent from many prehistoric cultures are slender. Murdoch (1957) compiled a list of cross-cultural constants from the ethnographic literature. Of relevance to child development was a basic mother–child unit but immense variety of other aspects of the family. Of course some kind of socially-recognized kinship system was another constant. Ideas of relatedness and family are regarded by many anthropologists as the core and key to human social organization. There may be cross-cultural constants at other levels of description or analysis. Eibl-Eibesfeldt (1972), and Ekman *et al.* (1969) have described extensive similarities in facial expressions and non-verbal communications in a wide range of different and isolated cultures. Hall, Chisholm, Woodson and Blurton Jones devised a descriptive list of observable behaviour of mother and baby. This has been used, with only the smallest modification, in several cultures (Chisholm: Navajo; Woodson: Malay, Tamil, Chinese; Hall: London Working Class) and it is hard for us to imagine a culture in which this list would not cover most of what mothers, and babies up to two years old, do with each other. We have yet to complete analyses of how the bits of behaviour fit together. This is where we would begin to find a mixture of similarities and differences across cultures (Chisholm, in press).

QUANTITATIVE COMPARATIVE STUDIES

When ethologists began to tire of running riotously through the animal kingdom pointing out similarities between human and animal behaviour some of us tried to settle down to a more reliable quantitative use of the comparative method. This is now widely used in animal behaviour and comparative functional anatomy but could be used more than it has to make some deductions about the behaviour of early man.

One example is a compilation that I made (Blurton Jones, 1972) of information about milk composition and mammalian child-rearing practices (Ben Shaul, 1962) and about mammalian sucking rates (Wolff, 1968). Ben Shaul showed, from her sample of about 100 species, that gross aspects of milk composition were not related to taxonomic position but to the patterns of mother–offspring contact, particularly the interval between feeds. Species that feed their young at wide intervals, such as rabbits (a feed every 24 hours), tree shrews (48 hours) had the highest fat and protein content. Those that fed their young most often, species in which the young ride on their mother (or in her pouch) and feed very frequently, have the lowest fat and protein levels in their milk. I found that Wolff's data correlate well with those of Ben Shaul. Species with widely spaced feeds have the fastest rates of sucking (within a bout of sucking). As it happens their feeds are very short, probably because of the risk of attracting predators to their nest or hiding place. Perhaps this is why they suck so fast. The slowest rates of sucking are found in species with constant contact and low fat and protein content of the milk. If we look at the composition of human milk, and babies' sucking rate within bouts of sucking, we can extrapolate the frequency of feeding. Human mothers and babies are at the extreme end of the distribution, at the frequent feeding, continuous contact end. Other details are involved (see Blurton Jones, 1972) but this is a fairly strong comparative argument that for significant lengths of human prehistory mother and baby were together all the time. Note that it is not evidence that they were secluded or stationary. This pattern occurs mainly in mammals where the young follow mother from birth (obviously babies cannot do this), or where the baby is carried on mother's body (in Callithicidae on father also). Since our closest relatives, the great apes, also carry their babies it seems a safe bet that carrying babies has been a continuous habit right back to our higher primate ancestors.

Perhaps other aspects of child-rearing can be investigated in this way. The length of contact between mother and baby is one that might be worth investigating. I think it relates to the variety of foods and foraging patterns that the species uses, as well as to being social.

CONTEMPORARY HUNTER–GATHERERS

Several hunting and gathering cultures survived into this century. A number have useful ethnographies, a few still exist and may continue to be studied as they meet and merge with the agricultural, iron-using majority. Although a common core of characteristics has been discerned, there are differences between these cultures. This must not be forgotten when we consider the child-rearing literature, which comes overwhelmingly from one such culture, arguably a good choice but not the only choice.

Lee and DeVore (1968) set out their now familiar argument about the importance of hunter–gatherer people for our understanding of human evolution. More than 99% of human generations lived a hunting and gathering way of life. Thus to the extent that evolution has shaped us, it is the selection pressures of a hunting and gathering way of life that shaped us. Of course the details of a way of life depend on the environment. Lee (1968) showed that even a single variable like the proportion of animal food in the diet of hunter–gatherer peoples varied markedly with latitude. DeVore argues that the fossil evidence suggests that for most of human evolution the species was confined to old world tropical savannah. This is the argument in favour of taking the best documented hunter–gatherer society, the !kung Bushmen of Botswana and Namibia studied by the Marshalls and by a team of anthropologists headed by DeVore (Lee, 1980; Lee and DeVore, 1976), as important and relevant. But it is essential to remember that other populations, such as the Hadza in their richer savannah environment in western Tanzania (Woodburn, 1968), show differences from, as well as similarities to, the Bushmen.

Detailed studies of !kung Bushmen child-rearing have been carried out by Draper (1976) and by Konner (1972, 1976). Of particular interest are two review papers by Konner and colleagues (Konner, 1975; West and Konner, 1976). Both Konner and Draper are still working on their full accounts of !kung infancy and childhood respectively but some clear points are worth mentioning here.

In the case of the early relationship between mother and baby the information from all described hunter–gatherer societies agrees with the comparative evidence for constant contact between mother and child and frequent feeding. Indeed in the !kung Bushmen, Konner found that the average interval between feeds was 13 minutes. Konner and Worthman (1980) showed that inter-feed interval was correlated with serum estradiol and progesterone levels and suggested that frequency of suckling was an important aspect of the suppression of ovulation by breast feeding.

Konner (1975) showed that in any hunter–gatherer group children would seldom be able to play with more than one or two age mates. Most of their potential playmates would be older or younger than themselves. Most of the time that Bushmen children spent with other children was with children of differing ages. Hold (1980) found that Gwi Bushmen children also played in mixed age groups but showed a preference toward interacting with children of their own age. These findings make a startling contrast to the various pre-school groups into which we put so much effort, money and propaganda. Of course within these very unnatural settings many children make themselves a natural situation of a handful of actual playmates. However, Blurton Jones and Konner (1973) argued that this freedom of choice might be one factor in the development of the more extensive sex differences that they found in London children than in Bushmen children.

West and Konner (1976) reviewed the evidence about father

participation in infant care. Their main conclusion is that our stereo-type of the primeval "Victorian *pater familias*" is an erroneous picture of hunter–gatherer fatherhood. While mothers may have always done more with babies than fathers have, nonetheless fathers may have done a lot of baby care during our evolutionary past. Indeed comparative arguments can be deduced for the view that human fathers are adapted to show a great deal more direct child care than are any other higher primate fathers, resembling the baby-carrying Callithicid father more than the briefly bemusedly tolerant baboon or gorilla father. An entirely different kind of analysis of Bushman ecology by Blurton Jones and Sibly (1978) may also imply that a hunter–gatherer father may be able to make an immense contribution to his reproductive success just by baby-sitting while his wife goes gathering plant foods.

Draper and Konner both characterize Bushman child-rearing as indulgent and responsive. Parents are available to infants and children but not intrusive. Children are not organized into responsibilities like child care. Much can be made of this by those who favour a permissive nurturing kind of education. But at a time when many are turning away from that approach to education it would be nice to have more direct evidence about the long-term results of each approach to child-rearing and education. In our longitudinal study in London my research group has added to the growing evidence that contingent response by parents is as important or more important than sheer frequency of interaction. Later in this paper we show how mothers' readiness to follow the child's lead in sociable interactions leads to higher scores in developmental tests. We have also found that mothers who respond readily to their toddlers crying (in accidents, not in disputes) have children whose interactions with other children are less aggressive and more sociable, and who have fewer problems at school reported by their teacher. On the other hand we have shown that, as many people would expect, mothers who more often approach their child when it is one or two years old (clingy mothers?) are likely to end up with the more clingy three-year-olds, who protest about mother leaving the room, and stay nearer her while she is in the room, when compared with other children. So perhaps we are beginning to see evidence that the sort of child-rearing that, as well as we can tell, hunter–gatherers went in for, indeed works well for contemporary children (I am reminded of my first impression of a Bushman dry season village: "what a perfect situation in which to rear children". I quickly realized that this was backwards, this is the kind of situation to which children's development was fitted by evolution).

However Whiten (in press), comparing rural African agriculturalist child-rearing with British child-rearing, has pointed out the huge differences in the levels of technology that our children have to get to grips with. We cannot unquestioningly expect the environment of evolutionary adaptedness to be able to promote that sort of learning. However, the high technology hunter–gatherer societies like eastern arctic eskimos might have something to teach us here.

The most striking feature of Bushman child-rearing, that pinpoints more striking and dependable deviations from the environment of evolutionary adaptedness, is the situation of mothers. Being a mother in Bushman society does not remove one from social, political and economic life as it tends to do in urban industrial society. Home, for instance in a dry season camp, is the centre in which everything happens. Hunting or gathering excursions start and end there, the groups of people concerned return there with their gains, talk over the day's proceedings there, discuss plans and working, economic and social relationships there. There is nothing about having children that interferes with these activities. The contrast with the urban mother and child could not be stronger. Mother and child stay at home, most of the money is earned elsewhere, by father. Most of the relatives live elsewhere. Friends are dispersed in their own separate houses. Political and economic events happen away from home. Father has a separate working society away from home. Mother may or may not have a social network happening around home. It does not take too much imagination to connect this with some of the problems of women with small children, and with the contradictions and opposing loyalties felt by mothers who wish to work.

DO THE DIFFERENCES BETWEEN CONTEMPORARY CHILD-REARING AND PREHISTORIC CHILD-REARING MATTER?

We have already touched on this issue in discussing the evidence from contemporary hunter–gatherers. In general, one may be tempted to suppose that deviations from an evolved system could have far-reaching consequences. If a complex mechanism is asked to function outside the ranges for which it was designed one might expect wild and bizarre results. But this is not a necessary conclusion: we should be on the look-out for trouble but we cannot be sure there will be trouble. In addition, an organism that can cope with a range of environments is likely to do better on an evolutionary time scale than one which cannot. So we cannot approach this question with any certain expectations.

Let us confine attention to three topics: (1) unnaturally large peer groups, (2) deviations from constant contact between mother and child, (3) the isolation of urban mothers.

Several studies have tried to look for effects of pre-school experience of large peer groups. Some have found no difference related to length of pre-school or day care experience, some have claimed to show more aggression, less adult-centred behaviour, and changed patterns of attachment in children with longer day care or pre-school experience. These findings suggest that the deviation from the environment of evolutionary adaptedness might indeed have consequences that some would regard as detrimental. Most of these studies have taken care to control for major background variables such as social class and birth order. The studies vary greatly in the daily period of substitute care being investigated, from a couple of hours in a small playgroup, to ten hours or more in a day nursery. This might be a very important variable. However, our longitudinal study gives another reason to reserve judgment on most of the existing studies. We found that the amount of pre-school playgroup or nursery school experience the children were going to get could be predicted from their behaviour and that of their mother *before* they started pre-school. Children who started pre-school at a young age and thus ended up with more experience of pre-school were *already* more independent, interacted more with children than adults and were more aggressive *before* they started going to pre-school. On balance it looks as if children are amazingly unperturbed by the double unnaturalness of separation from mother and accompaniment by large number of age mates.

Do deviations from constant contact of mother and infant in the early months matter? The well-known findings by Kennel *et al.* (1974; Klaus and Kennel, 1976) about early contact, now several times replicated, look very much like one way in which it might matter. At least for some mothers this early contact seems very important. Woodson (1980) as described later in this paper, has argued that it may matter for the physiology of the baby, with possible long-term consequences in extreme cases. McKeith (1969), Jelliffe and Jelliffe (1978) and others have documented differences in physical health of babies that are bottle fed. The physical consequences of this difference from the evolved pattern remain more convincing than any psychological differences.

The striking contrast between the social and economic situation of urban mothers and hunter–gatherer mothers surely has something to do with current findings about correlates of depression of women. Brown *et al.* (1975) found that those most at risk were working-class mothers of young children, who did not have a job outside the home. He suggested that middle-class mothers might be protected by being better at arranging a fuller social life, and time away from the children, as indeed Gavron (1965) showed that they were. The ways of coping with the situation entail further unnatural situations — day care or nursery school for the children. At best urban mothers are thrown into a mesh of unsatisfactory attempts at solutions to the unnatural situation they are placed in. Thus, we were pleased to find in our longitudinal study of working-class families that, although unsatisfactory social contacts with kin and others were important predictors of postnatal and toddlerhood depression in women, the traditional working-class matriarchy described by Young and Willmott (1957) still exists. The majority of women seem to get valuable support from their mothers and other kin. In her analyses of maternal depression in our study, Susan Pollock (in preparation) also demonstrated a contribution of characteristics of the baby to predicting maternal depression. As you might expect, but no-one had tested the probabilities before, difficult babies got depressed mothers. There was an important upsurge of depression at the end of the first year after the birth. This is the time when difficult newborns turn into night-waking toddlers (Richards, 1977; Blurton Jones et al., 1978; Pollock et al., in press). Our habit of separating parent and child at night then conspires with the aforementioned deviations from our environment of evolutionary adaptedness to make life intolerable for a significant proportion of mothers of one-year-old children.

The Child's Influence on the Environment in which it Develops

Ideas in this arena range from the simple observation that behaviour of newborn babies provokes response from parents, through to more complex propositions such as Bateson's (1976) suggestion that behavioural analogues of catch-up growth may exist, that the infant contains a development organizing system that (at least) is able to return it to a normal course of development after some events have disturbed its development. This idea is compatible with findings in developmental psychology, emphasized by Clarke and Clarke (1976). Recovery from early setbacks seem to be the rule rather than the exception. The belief in irreversible early influences that was the fashion in developmental psychology a few years ago has been overturned. No doubt both views could have done with more relevant data and less bandwaggoning. The evidence for irreversible early influences was never very strong in the behaviour of relatively normal healthy children. Much of it was based on the observation of early as well as late differences in the behaviour of children of different social classes. The enduring differences in the situation of the children were overlooked.

Mary Ainsworth (1970) and John Bowlby (1969) have written about the infant's contribution to developing its attachment to its mother, though Ainsworth seems to attribute most of the variation in patterns of attachment to variation in mother's response to the child. Another influential paper was that by Bell (1968) and this paper should have still more influence. The central point was that since we know that the behaviour of babies differs between individuals in the first hours after birth we cannot assume that correlations between behaviour of parent and child are evidence of effects of parent on child. They may just as well be effects of child on parent. Indeed we cannot even maintain the old pre-Bell assumptions for cross-cultural differences. Freedman (1971) has shown that populations of newborn babies differ in their behaviour and Chisholm (1978) has shown that differences between Navajo and Anglo mother–infant interactions are greatest in the newborn period and are attributable to differences in the behaviour of the babies, and that the differences in mother–infant interaction decrease and disappear by the end of the first year of life. Obviously, many and massive cross-cultural differences (and individual differences) do not arise from difficulties in the baby but from ideas and circumstances of the parents. It is also conceivable that differences in behaviour of babies in the first hours are a result of differences in the way they are handled. But, even so, there is clearly no longer any excuse for the blind assumption that an association between parental behaviour and child behaviour can be taken as evidence of an effect of parent on child without further evidence of the possible contributions of the child to the correlation. Of course development is probably a tangle (or if we agree with Bateson, a complex system) of effects in each direction. Baby may affect mother who may affect baby, and so on. But the task for researchers on child-rearing is clearly to try to understand these networks of interactions and perhaps to disentangle them and demonstrate the existence of each component.

Blurton Jones et al. (1979) published a description of one such theoretical network of influences that had some effects similar to the self-righting system Bateson was proposing. In this instance the feedback was between child and parent and not within the child. I will now describe an ongoing project in which a model much closer to Bateson's is being tested, in the newborn period, and then describe an analysis of behaviour of one- to two-year-old children that looks very close to a demonstration that the child can arrange for itself an environment that is helpful for development.

ADAPTIVE BEHAVIOUR BY THE NEWBORN

The newborn study was devised by R. Woodson, and is being carried out by Woodson and H. Morgan at the Institute of Obstetrics and Gynaecology under the direction of Geoffrey Chamberlain and myself and is funded by the Mental Health Foundation. Following from his earlier work on the relationship between perinatal events and newborn behaviour in one of our longitudinal studies, and doubtless influenced by views expressed earlier by Freedman and by Chisholm (but independently from the excitingly similar outlook of G. Anderson Shankland (1977)) Woodson proposed that the behaviour of newborn babies should be looked at as part of the evolved homeostatic system of the baby. The function of newborn behaviour would be to aid the baby's physiology in getting the internal environment to normal levels, after the disruption of birth, and through the normal changes from fetal to postnatal life. If it was an evolved system it must be adapted to work only in a certain range of environments, and in particular only in a certain range of child-rearing practices. The most obvious simple example is blood sugar levels. If low sugar makes babies cry and crying results in mother feeding baby (as it frequently does even in our culture) then sugar levels will be brought up again. Woodson argues that this sort of feedback loop goes much further than just hunger (indeed it is not even clear that hunger works as one would imagine in the first few days). The literature on newborn physiology shows that many important measures of the internal environment are linked and suggests that several of these are influenced directly or indirectly by a feed, and differently for breast and bottle feeds. At the same time it is clear that behaviour such as crying has some direct and costly effects on the internal environment. It obviously uses a lot of energy, may increase heat loss by the accompanying changes in posture and flushing, and it has effects on pO_2 (Anderson, 1977). The costs of crying will differ for a warm baby and a cold baby, but so will the risks of not crying. The exact circumstances in which it would pay a baby to cry or not cry (pay in terms of most benefit to its survival chances) will clearly differ by small and intricate margins. It is thus surprising that evidence exists (Graham, 1957; Woodson et al., 1981) that low blood pH is associated with more crying but not surprising that the clinical impression should evolve that irritable babies had been somewhat asphyxiated but that "flat" babies had been much more badly affected. The costs of crying may outweigh the benefits in the unhealthy baby as well as in the contented baby.

At first glance, crying may appear to be among the least useful behaviours in which a newborn who has experienced asphyxia could engage. The blood pO2 drops dramatically during bouts of crying (Anderson, 1977). Forceful crying with increased muscular activity substantially raises oxygen consumption, in some cases resulting in a fourfold increase over the basal rate (Cross *et al.*, 1957). As well as consuming energy substrates, the increased metabolic activity associated with crying would result in the creation of metabolic acids. These outcomes could hardly be beneficial to a newborn who is already acidotic, liable to become hypoxic and whose metabolic reserves are likely to be depleted as a result of asphyxia (Shelley, 1969).

This conclusion is based upon observations of the newborn left alone and allowed to cry. In the natural environment, however, crying elicits a prompt response from the mother. The components of this response, moreover, are quite specific: the newborn who cries is very likely to be picked up, held closely and continually against the mother's body and fed (Bell and Ainsworth, 1972; Brazelton, 1972; Konner, 1976). A rather different set of consequences become apparent when crying is viewed from this perspective.

It can be inferred from the experimental evidence that contact with the mother's warm body will reduce heat loss, promote thermal stability and lessen the thermogenic demands confronting the newborn (Adamsons, 1966; Silverman *et al.*, 1966; Hey and Katz, 1970). It is known that recovery from acidosis is enhanced if the newborn is kept in a constantly warm environment (Gandy *et al.*, 1964). Along with its contribution to acid-base regulation, the reduction in metabolic activity afforded by thermal stability would also lessen the risk of hypoglycaemia (Hull, 1974).

Feeding obviously provides nutrients and fluids but two additional benefits derived from nursing at the breast warrant special mention with respect to the asphyxiated newborn. First, because its metabolism gives rise to few acid end-products, breast milk enables the newborn to obtain nourishment at a minimum additional burden to renal capacity (McCance and Widdowson, 1960; Fomon *et al.*, 1959). Secondly, it has been shown that non-nutritive sucking facilitates oxygenation in transitional premature newborns (Burroughs *et al.*, 1978). Thus, the opportunity to nurse in and of itself may be beneficial for the maintenance of adequate respiratory function.

So the mother's responses to crying appear to promote adequate ventilation, assist in recovery from acidosis and ensure a balance between metabolic demands and reserves — three recognized goals in the treatment of asphyxia (Keay and Morgan, 1978). Thus, to the extent that it elicits caretaking responses that promote homeostasis, crying may be viewed as a means of using the postnatal environment to compensate for the effects of previous insult.

The clinical treatments which have so dramatically reduced the risk of death and disablement during the perinatal period must be recognized as recent developments. Yet the factors that complicate the transition to extra-uterine life have presumably done so throughout the history of the human species. Contemporary medicine did not invent asphyxia, only the means to measure it and improved ways to cope with it.

Thus, until relatively recently, the only special care unit in which recovery from perinatal complications could take place was the environment provided and staffed by the mother. This is the environment in which patterns of interaction characteristic of the human mother and newborn have evolved and are designed to function. It is reasonable to assume that the need to make good less-than-optimal fetal experiences has been among the strongest of the selective pressures that have shaped these patterns.

So Woodson is proposing that there is an intricately adapted series of links from the newborn's internal environment to its behaviour, to mother's responses and from these back to its internal environment. In talking of nature's special care unit he is not challenging the superiority of medicine's special care unit for the unwell or small baby, but he is implying something very important for those of us interested in the care and development of the normal and well babies. Neonatologists have shown that special care units can determine whether or not extreme low birth-weight leads to later problems. In the same way Woodson's model implies that in the normal baby, whether minor perinatal problems have later consequences will depend not only on how well the environment compensates later—see Sameroff and Chandler's important review (1975)—but also on how effective the newborn's behaviour is at getting its internal environment on to normal values. It would thus be hard to attribute any associations that sometimes appear (they usually do, but not always, depending on your outcome measures among other things) between perinatal events and later development or behaviour, purely to the physiological events or to the mother's handling. The proposition is that baby is leading mother towards helping it sort out its internal environment. If later consequences have a physiological basis they can be avoided by mother following baby's lead. The trade-off may of course be that mother is taught some bad habits, which in turn influence the child. Indeed it may be that kind of chain of interaction that determines whether or not perinatal events within the normal range have any consequences.

This is not a proposition that should be taken up too quickly by propagandists for natural child care. Brazelton (1972) pointed out how in a culture where demand feeding was the norm, a baby that did not cry (perhaps because too ill or too starved) got dangerously underfed. The silent baby might be doing the best it can, merely because the other options might kill it quicker and because there is always a chance (probably growing with time!) that mother may decide it needs feeding.

Woodson's theory is one that demands measurement and experiment on causes and consequences of behaviour, which could then lead to the calculation of optimal behaviour for various physiological situations, followed by further observation to see if the behaviour that occurs is indeed optimal. This process of quantification, hypothesis construction and test is attractive to scientists but not conducive to instant belief and application. Its weakest point is the assumption about the effects of baby behaviour on maternal behaviour in the environment of evolutionary adaptedness. I discussed the ways one can partly tighten such assumptions in an earlier section. The beauty of Woodson's theory as a theory that demonstrates a total interdependence of biological and social influences on child development should be obvious.

THE TODDLER ARRANGES ITS SOCIAL ENVIRONMENT

It has become commonplace in studies of the earliest part of language development to suggest that the child's gestures are an important part of the process. By gesturing the child seems to provoke responses from its mother which may in turn play a part in further development of communication and language. Surprisingly little effort has been made to measure and test this proposition. One such effort comes from our longitudinal study of sixty middle-class firstborn children (and we hope to follow it up with analysis of data from our longitudinal study of working-class children). The longitudinal study was done by M. C. R. Ferreira, Marilyn Brown, Lynne Moore and myself and supported by SSRC Project Grant HR1745. It illustrates one possible approach to charting the mutual influences of child on parent and parent on child. It comes near to demonstrating one way in which children can provoke their parents into providing a helpful environment (obviously parents will differ in how easily they are provoked, as we shall see).

Several research workers have found that aspects of children's early language development can be predicted by mother's response to the child's vocalization (Nelson, 1973; Clarke-Stewart, 1973; Lieven,

1978; Davis, 1978). Following Stella (1974) we found that in our sample, contemporaneous and subsequent test scores were predicted by the proportion of child utterances (that were not crying, fretting, laughing, screaming, imitations of motor vehicles, fire engine sirens, etc, i.e. speech-like vocalizations) that led immediately to mother speaking to child (not prohibitions or criticisms). Mothers who answered more of the child's utterances (when we observed them at 15 months and 21 months old) had children who scored higher in tests (at 21 months when first tested and subsequently).

One's natural assumption might be that this correlation implies that mother's response aids language development. But even if we leave aside the question of what else about mother's speech might be more important, we ought to ask whether the finding might not instead result from immediate influences of child on mother. Is it not easier to answer a child who talks well? Are there other things done by children who later score high in tests that might make mother more likely to respond? If there are, they may completely explain away the association between mother's readiness to respond and child's test scores. If taking them into account does not remove the association between response and test score, then we are as near as we can get to demonstrating a case where the child provokes behaviour from mother which has a demonstrated effect on the child's development.

Let me discuss only one example that we investigated. When one-year-old children speak they often point at an object, or hold out the object towards mother, offering or showing it to her. Perhaps this draws mother's attention to the child, and makes it clear what the child is talking about. One can imagine this making it easier to give the mother's commonest response: repeat a word the child seemed to say, and add a word of praise. In our sample it was true that children who did well in the language tests also did more proffering and pointing to mother in the observations. It was also true that mother was more likely to respond to vocalizations accompanied by point and proffer than unaccompanied vocalizations. Thus it is quite reasonable to propose that the child's proffering might explain away the correlation between mother's response and child's test score. We looked at this possibility in two ways, one a sledgehammer statistical approach, the other a more simple commonsense approach, though they are basically the same. In the first method we entered rate of proffer and point first in a regression equation predicting test score, then we entered mother's response to see if its contribution had been removed. It had not. Thus, statistically controlling for frequency of proffering fails to explain away the correlation between mother's response and child's test score. The second approach gave the same result. We derived two new scores: (a) the proportion of utterance *with* proffer and point that led to mother speaking to child and (b) the proportion of utterances *without* proffer and point that led to mother speaking to child. As indicated already, score (a) was much higher than score (b). If proffering was to explain away the original correlation, no correlation should remain between either of these new scores, and test score. Yet it did. Indeed the proportion of proffer and point leading to mother-speak-to-child gives the strongest and most predicting score we have for language scores and IQ test scores. It predicts the early language test scores, and thus disproves the hypothesis that our original correlation was due merely to it being easier to answer children who talk well because they proffer and point a lot. But it also predicts IQ test scores (Stanford-Binet, often thought of as very language dependent) at three, four and five years old. (A word of warning: this is impressive but such a finding does *not* demonstrate a lasting effect on the child: mother's response to her one-year-old's point and proffer may be a good predictor of later mother behaviour that in turn determines later test scores.)

So mother's rate of response to speech-like utterances, with and without gesturing, predicts language test scores. It remains possible that this aspect of mother's behaviour actually promotes language development. Other aspects may do so also; we must test whether those are actually more important than her answering. But meanwhile, since gesturing clearly increases mother's rate of answering we have data that are very close to a demonstration that by gesturing the child does indeed provoke from its mother behaviour that helps its language development. This is an idea that originated from theories about the infant as an evolved, active partner in its development, became a near dogma in some parts of developmental psychology but seldom received any quantitative testing.

Conclusion

There are other analyses of this type that we have made of our data, and Richards and his colleagues have made of their longitudinal data, that suggest even stronger influences of the child on its environment. One example has already been mentioned above. The age at which the children start nursery school could be predicted from the behaviour in playroom observations a year or so earlier. The independent sociable children started earlier. Other studies noting correlations of preschool experience and behaviour found it hard to resist the conclusion that preschool influences behaviour. But it seems that even three-year-olds can be self-selected samples. Obviously these influences will always occur in .interaction with other factors. Mother's behaviour may be determined partly by her child's behaviour and partly by her situation. The direction of the effect of her child's behaviour might even be reversed by her circumstances. But it is clear that we can no longer think of mother (or father) as the only contributors to the relationship. They may be the ones we can reason with but we should remember that they may be dealing with a baby who has been powerfully selected to have its say, and who may not fit our ideas of what a mother ought to be able to get from her baby. Impractical advice is seldom taken. In the field of baby care most impractical advice comes from underestimating the extent and persistence of differences between babies, and the power of their influence on interactions with other people.

References

Adamsons, K. (1966). The role of the thermal factors in fetal and neonatal life. *Pediatrics Clinics of North America*, **13**, 599–619.

Anderson, G. C. (1977). The mother and newborn: mutual caregivers. *Journal of Obstetric, Gynecologic and Neonatal Nursing*, **6**, 50–57.

Ainsworth, M. D. S. (1970). Object relations, dependency, and attachment: a theoretical review of the infant–mother relationship. *Child Development*, **40**, 969–1026.

Bateson, P. P. G. (1976). Rules and reciprocity in behavioural development. In *Growing Points in Ethology*. Edited by P. P. G. Bateson and R. A. Hinde. Cambridge: Cambridge University Press.

Bell, R. Q. (1968). A reinterpretation of the direction of effects in studies of socialization. *Psychological Review*, **75**, 81–95.

Bell, S. M. and Ainsworth, M. D. S. (1972). Infant crying and maternal responsiveness. *Child Development*, **43**, 1171–1190.

Ben Shaul, D. M. (1962). The composition of the milk of wild animals. *International Zoo Year Book*, **4**, 333–342.

Blurton Jones, N. G. (1972). Comparative aspects of mother–child contact. In *Ethological Studies of Child Behaviour*. Edited by N. G. Blurton Jones. Cambridge: Cambridge University Press.

Blurton Jones, N. G., Ferreira, M. C. Rossetti, Brown, M. Farquhar, and Macdonald, L. (1978). The association between perinatal factors and later night waking. *Developmental Medicine and Child Neurology*, **20**, 427–434.

Blurton Jones, N. G. and Konner, M. J. (1973). Sex differences in behaviour of London and Bushman children. In *Comparative Ecology and Behaviour of Primates*. Edited by R. P. Michael and J. H. Crook. London: Academic Press.

Blurton Jones, N. G. and Sibly, R. M. (1978). Testing adaptiveness of culturally determined behaviour: do Bushman women maximize their reproductive success by spacing births widely and foraging seldom? In *Human Behaviour and Adaptation*. Edited by V. Reynolds and N. Blurton Jones. London: Taylor and Francis.

Blurton Jones, N. G., Woodson, R. H. and Chisholm, J. S. (1979). Cross-cultural perspectives on the significance of social relationships in infancy. In *The First Year of Life*. Edited by H. R. Shaffer and J. Dunn. New York and Chichester, Sussex: John Wiley and Sons.

Bowlby, J. (1969). *Attachment and Loss*. Vol. 1 *Attachment*. London: Hogarth Press.

Brazelton, T. B. (1972). Implications of infant development among the Mayan Indians of Mexico. *Human Development*, **15**, 90–111.

Brown, G. W., Bhrolchain, M. N., Harris, T. (1975). Social class and psychiatric disturbance among women in an urban population. *Sociology*, **9**, 225–254.

Burroughs, A. K., Asoyne, U. O., Anderson-Shanklin, G. C. and Vidyasagar, D. (1978). The effect of non-nutritive sucking on transcutaneous oxygen tension in non-crying, preterm neonates. *Research in Nursing and Health*, **1**, 69–75.

Chisholm, J. S. (1978). *Developmental Ethology of the Navajo*. Ph.D. Thesis, Rutgers University, New Jersey.

Chisholm, J. S. (in press). Residence patterns and the environment of mother–infant interaction among the Navajo. In *Culture and Early Interactions*. Edited by T. Field *et al.* Hillsdale, New Jersey: Lawrence Erlbaum Associates.

Clarke, A. M. and Clarke, A. D. B. (1976). *Early Experience: Myth and Evidence*. London: Open Books; New York: Free Press.

Clarke-Stewart, K. A. (1973). Interactions between mothers and their young children: characteristics and consequences. *Monographs of the Society for Research in Child Development 38* No. 153.

Cross, K. W., Tizard, J. P. and Trythall, D. A. (1957). The gaseous metabolism of the newborn infant. *Acta Paediatrica*, **46**, 265–285.

Davis, H. (1978). A description of aspects of mother–infant vocal interaction. *Journal of Child Psychology and Psychiatry*, **19**, 379–386.

Draper, P. (1976). Social and economic constraints on child life among the !kung. In *Kalahari Hunter-Gatherers*. Edited by R. B. Lee and I. DeVore. Cambridge, Massachusetts and London: Harvard University Press.

Eibl-Eibesfeldt, I. (1972). Similarities and differences between cultures in expressive movements. In *Non-Verbal Communication*. Edited by R. A. Hinde. Cambridge: Cambridge University Press.

Ekman, P., Sorenson, E. R. and Friesen, W. V. (1969). Pan-cultural elements in facial displays of emotion. *Science*, **164**, 86–88.

Fomon, S. J., Harris, D. M. and Jensen, R. L. (1959). Acidification of the urine by infants fed human milk and whole cow's milk. *Paediatrics*, **23**, 113–119.

Freedman, D. G. (1971). Genetic influences on development of behavior. In *Normal and Abnormal Development of Brain*. Edited by G. B. A. Stoelinga and J. J. Werff ten Bosch. Leiden: Leiden University Press; Baltimore: Williams and Wilkins.

Gandy, G. M., Adamsons, K., Cunningham, N., Silverman, W. and James, L. S. (1964). Thermal environment and acid-base homeostasis in human infants during the first few hours of life. *Journal of Clinical Investigations*, **43**, 751–758.

Gavron, H. (1965). *The Captive Wife*. London: Routledge and Kegan Paul.

Graham, F. K., Rennoyev, M. M., Caldwell, B. M., Greenman, M. and Hartsan, A. F. (1957). Relationship between clinical status and behavior test performance in a newborn group with histories suggesting anoxia. *Journal of Pediatrics*, **50**, 177.

Hamilton, W. D. (1964). The genetical evolution of social behaviour. *Journal of Theoretical Biology*, **7**, 1–16.

Harpending, H. (1980). Perspectives on the theory of social evolution. In *Current Developments in Anthropological Genetics*. Edited by J. Mielke, and M. Crawford. New York and London: Plenum Press.

Hey, E. N. and Katz, G. (1970). The optimum thermal environment for naked babies. *Archives of Diseases in Childhood*, **45**, 328–334.

Hold, B. (1980). Attention-structure and behavior in G/wi San children. *Ethology and Sociobiology*, **1**, 275–290.

Hull, D. (1974). The function and development of adipose tissue. In *Scientific Foundations of Paediatrics*. Edited by J. A. Davis and J. Dobbing. London: Heinemann.

Jelliffe, D. B. and Jelliffe, E. F. P. (1978). *Human Milk in the Modern World; Psychosocial, Nutritional and Economic Significance*. Oxford: Oxford University Press.

Keay, A. J. and Morgan, D. M. (1978). *Craig's Care of the Newly Born Infant* (Sixth Edition), Edinburgh: Churchill Livingstone.

Kennell, J. H., Jerauld, R., Wolfe, H., Chester, D., Kreger, N., McAlpine, W., Steffa, M. and Klaus, M. H. (1974). Maternal behaviour one year after early and extended post-partum contact. *Developmental Medicine and Child Neurology*, **16**, 172–179.

Klaus, M. H. and Kennell, J. H. (1976). Maternal–infant bonding. The impact of early separation or loss on family development. St. Louis, CV Mosby Co.

Konner, M. J. (1972). Aspects of the developmental ethology of a foraging people. In *Ethological Studies of Child Behaviour*. Edited by N. G. Blurton Jones. Cambridge: Cambridge University Press.

Konner, M. J. (1975). Relations among infants and juveniles in comparative perspectives. In *Friendship and Peer Relations*. Edited by M. Lewis and L. A. Rosenblum. New York and Chichester, Sussex: John Wiley and Sons.

Konner, M. J. (1976). Maternal care, infant behavior, and development among the Zhun/twa (!kung) bushmen. In *Kalahari Hunter-Gatherers*. Edited by R. B. Lee and I. DeVore. Cambridge, Massachusetts and London: Harvard University Press.

Konner, M. J. and Worthman, C. (1980). Nursing frequency, gonadal function, and birth-spacing among !kung hunter-gatherers. *Science*, **207**, 788–791.

Lee, R. B. (1968). What hunters do for a living, or, how to make out on scarce resources. In *Man the Hunter*. Edited by R. B. Lee, and I. DeVore. Chicago: Aldine.

Lee, R. B. (1980). *The !kung San. Men, Women, and Work in a Foraging Society*. Cambridge: Cambridge University Press.

Lee, R. B. and DeVore, I. (1968). *Man the Hunter*. Chicago: Aldine.

Lee, R. B. and DeVore, I. (1976). *Kalahari Hunter-Gatherers*. Cambridge, Massachusetts and London: Harvard University Press.

Lieven, E. V. M. (1978). Conversations between mothers and young children: individual differences and their possible implication for the study of language learning. In *The Development of Communication: Social and Pragmatic Factors in Language Acquisition*. Edited by N. Waterson and C. Snow. Chichester, Sussex and New York: John Wiley and Sons.

McCance, R. A. and Widdowson, E. M. (1960). Renal aspects of acid-base control in the newly born. *Acta Paediatrica*, **149**, 409–420.

McKeith, R. C. (1969). Breast feed for the first two months. *Developmental Medicine and Child Neurology*, **11**, 277.

Murdock, G. P. (1957). World ethnographic sample. *American Anthropologist*, **59**, 664–687.

Nelson, K. (1973). Structure and strategy in learning to talk. *Monographs of the Society for Research in Child Development*, **38**, 149.

Parker, G. A. and Macnair, M. R. (1979). Models of parent–offspring conflict. I. Monogamy. *Animal Behaviour*, **26**, 97–110.

Pfeiffer, J. (1974). *The Emergence of Man*. New York and London: Harper and Row.

Pollock, S., Blurton Jones, N. G., Woodson, R. H., da Costa Woodson, E. and Evans, M. A. (in prep). Correlates of postnatal depression.

Richards, M. P. M. (1977). An ecological study of infant development in an urban setting in Britain. In *Culture and Infancy: Variations in the Human Experience*. Edited by P. H. Leidermann, S. R. Tulkin and A. Rosenfeld. New York and London: Academic Press.

Sameroff, A. J. and Chandler, M. J. (1975). Reproductive risk and the continuum of caretaking causality. In *Review of Child Development Research*. Edited by F. D. Horowitz, M. Hetherington, S. Scarr-Salapatek and G. Stegel, vol. 4, pt. 4 pp. 187–244. Chicago: University of Chicago Press.

Shelley, H. J. (1969). The metabolic responses of the foetus to hypoxia. *Journal of Obstetrics and Gynaecology of the British Commonwealth*, **76**, 1–15.

Silverman, W. A., Sinclair, J. C. and Agate, F. J. (1966). The oxygen cost of minor changes in the heat balance of small newborn infants. *Acta Paediatrica Scandinavica*, **55**, 294–300.

Stella, E. M. (1974). *A Field-Descriptive and Experimental Study of Verbal Behaviour in One-Year-Old Children*. Unpublished Ph.D. thesis, University of London.

Trivers, R. L. (1974). Parent–offspring conflict. *American Zoologist*, **14**, 249–264.

Washburn, S. L. (1961). *Social Life of Early Man*. Chicago: Aldine.

West, M. M. and Konner, M. J. (1976). The role of the father: an anthropological perspective. In *The Role of the Father in Child Development*. Edited by M. E. Lamb. New York and Chichester, Sussex: John Wiley and Sons.

Whiten, A. and Milner, P. (in press). The educational environments of Nigerian infants. In *Nigerian Children: Perspectives on Development*. Edited by V. Curran.

Wolff, P. H. (1968). Sucking patterns of infant mammals. *Brain, Behaviour and Evolution*, **1**, 254–367.

Woodburn, J. (1968). An introduction to Hadza ecology. In *Man the Hunter*. Edited by R. B. Lee and I. DeVore. Chicago: Aldine.

Woodson, R. H. (1980). *Antecedents of Individual Differences in the Behaviour of Human Newborns*. Ph.D. thesis. University of London.

Woodson, R. H., Reader, F., Shepherd, J. and Chamberlain, G. (1981). Blood pH and crying in the newborn infant. *Infant Behavior and Development*, **4**, 41–46.

Young, M. and Willmott, P. (1957). *Family and Kinship in East London*. London: Routledge and Kegan Paul. (Pelican Books, 1962).

Parenting in Stepfamilies

JACQUELINE BURGOYNE

Department of Applied Social Studies,
Sheffield City Polytechnic, Sheffield, England

and

DAVID CLARK

MRC Medical Sociology Unit,
Institute of Medical Sociology, Aberdeen, Scotland

During the past decade a variety of social scientific studies have appeared which focus upon variant patterns of child-bearing and child-rearing. In some cases these have tended to point to problematic aspects of life in, for example, motherless (George and Wilding, 1972) or fatherless (Marsden, 1973) families using a framework in which illegitimacy, marital breakdown and divorce are frequently portrayed as resulting in stressful and damaging family circumstances. Whilst certain writers have emphasized the *negative* consequences of variation, however, others have located, and in some cases championed, what they see to be a healthy pluralism of family forms (Rapoport *et al.*, 1977, 1981). Influenced by both of these perspectives we ourselves have become increasingly interested in one of the variant types — the stepfamily. Accordingly, within the context of a study of forty stepfamilies living in the Sheffield area, carried out between 1977 and 1979, we have tried to identify the dominant characteristics of step-family life in terms of both private experience and structural constraint. When our study began we were interested initially, therefore, in patterns of role relationship to be found within the stepfamily and the various tensions and difficulties which might derive from these. More optimistically, we were also eager to examine the potential for variation and innovation in kinship relations which the stepfamily might contain.

In the early part of the study we held to a belief that stepfamily life could somehow be considered as a discrete entity within the range of possible family types. Indeed, like many others before us, we sub-scribed to an implicit and ill-defined notion of the "normal", "unbroken" nuclear family which could be invoked at will and, where necessary, contrasted with the variant family type of our concern. "Normal family life" therefore provided a baseline and our interest lay in discovering, on the one hand, which aspects of life in the stepfamily departed from it and, on the other, which conformed.

Therein lay our problem. For within a very short space of time it became clear that our conception of "normal" family life was sociologically a non-starter. Even on purely empirical grounds there was little to guide us in the way of description or ethnography, save the useful, but dated, community studies and the unhelpful generalizations of family sociology textbooks. We therefore found ourselves continually falling back upon that most dangerous of sociological concepts: commonsense. Our sociological understanding of normal family life, we learned, was no more than the sum of our direct personal experience and observation of it: uncontrolled, unmeasured and fragmentary. The difficulty is not, of course, one which has deterred sociologists in the past, who like many other experts in the field of social relations have spoken of "the family" without any apparent need for clarification of conceptualization. Nor yet do we ourselves claim to have resolved the problem; our intention is merely to highlight it. What then do we mean by "normal family life" and, more specifically, what are the constituent elements of parenting as an activity within it?

According to one estimate, 80% of adults in England and Wales become parents (Busfield, 1974 p. 13). Yet despite the ubiquity of the experience, surprisingly little is known about why parents have children and the meanings, motivations, aspirations and goals which attach to it. Part of the problem, of course, is the taken-for-grantedness of parenthood. Adults who marry are expected to have children, and indeed to refrain from doing so, as Busfield points out, is almost to fail to become a family at all (Busfield, 1974). Of course, it is extremely difficult to distinguish between voluntary and involuntary parenthood or childlessness, but where a couple are *perceived* as being voluntarily childless, then considerable social pressures may be brought to bear to "normalize" their behaviour, i.e. have children. Those groups for whom child-bearing is healthy, desirable and natural however are themselves socially defined. As Macintyre (1976) has shown, so-called maternal instincts are regarded as normal and estimable among pregnant women who are married, but are considered deviant, abnormal and undesirable when found amongst those who are single and pregnant. It is this very normality-within-limits which creates a problem of explanation for the sociologist who wishes to understand the meanings attached to having children. On the one hand, simply to recount actors' motives in becoming parents may be to run the risk of producing a bland and unremarkable set of homiletic accounts. Alternatively, to concentrate on the ideologies of parenting which are produced by family experts may tell us more about public rhetoric and ideologies of family life than the experiences of parents themselves. And yet there is a relationship between the two, which is sustained in the complex interplay between parenting theory and practice. Within the context of the stepfamily, where such issues may be found writ large, we are seeking to make sense then, not only of a variant type, but also of a widespread, pervasive, but ill-understood social activity: bearing and rearing children.

The Impact of Demographic Change

Although children living in stepfamilies remain in a minority, as a result of recent changes in patterns of divorce and remarriage, their numbers are increasing. Unpublished data collated for us by the Office of Population Censuses and Surveys (OPCS), from its 1976 Family Formation Survey indicate that in 1976 7% of all children under sixteen were living with a stepparent (Dunnell, 1979). Whilst rates of remarriage amongst the widowed have remained fairly constant over the last ten years, the number of marriages in which one or both partners is divorced, has risen very rapidly. From his survey of recent trends in marriage and divorce, Leete concludes:

> "Considerably more than one-third of people now divorcing will ultimately remarry (although) remarriage rates tend to decline as the time of divorce recedes" (Leete, 1979, p. 6)

It is these marriages, therefore, which are responsible for the increase in extent of steprelationships. Interestingly, the trend has not merely aroused the interests of academics and policy-makers, but has also taken a firm hold in popular culture. Since our research began we have witnessed an increasing public recognition of the popularity of remarriage and have noted a proliferation of magazine and newspaper articles on steprelationships as well as the development of divorce and remarriage plots in a number of radio and television soap operas.

Yet despite the movement from mortality- to divorce-generated stepfamilies, many of the enduring stereotypes of steprelationships, for example Chambers Twentieth Century Dictionary definition of the stepmother as a "cruel and niggardly guardian", have their origins in an earlier period when stepparents "stepped in" to replace a dead parent. Literary illustrations of some of the pitfalls of such substitution are found, for example, in Mrs Gaskell's *Wives and Daughters* (1866) as well as in some, still popular, children's stories. Today, however, stepfamilies are most commonly the result of remarriage after divorce rather than death and there are important differences between the two types. A consideration of these differences is not only necessary for an adequate understanding of contemporary steprelationships, but also helps us to isolate some of the more taken-for-granted aspects of beliefs about "mothering" or "fathering" in our society.

When widowed parents remarry they are likely to be older than their divorced counterparts, and typically, will have spent a longer period as lone parents prior to remarriage. Their children are, therefore, likely to be older and may also have become used to the altered circumstances of the one-parent family, in which they may have had the undivided, if exhausted, attention of their now remarrying parent. The eldest child in such a situation may even occupy a quasi-adult role in the family group, which must be relinquished when the new stepparent appears, thereby firmly dividing the household once more into two generations of adults and children.

By contrast, registration statistics indicate that remarriage following *divorce* usually takes place expeditiously. There are, however, a number of problems in the interpretation of such figures. On the one hand we know from a variety of research, including our own, that the *de facto* duration of a marriage is usually shorter than its *de jure* duration (Chester, 1971; Thornes and Collard, 1979) but it is also clear that most of those who ultimately remarry will live in cohabiting partnerships beforehand and some of these are of many years' standing. Data from the OPCS Family Formation Survey suggest that one-third of all women in second or subsequent partnerships were cohabiting rather than married at the time of the survey. The divorced couples in our own study had lived together for about two years on average before they married, some whilst they awaited the finalization of divorce arrangements, others because they did not wish to remarry immediately, even when they were free to do so. This meant that most of the children in our study acquired a *de facto* stepparent prior to their parent's remarriage and often quite soon after the initial separation.

Stepparents who "step in" to replace a dead parent are, it appears, able to take on that role more fully than their counterparts who replace a divorced, non-custodial parent. Although both bereaved partners and their children may continue to idealize the dead parent in a way which inhibits the development of relationships in the new family unit, except where pathological bereavement states ensue, the inevitable processes of loss and mourning usually ensure that such feelings gradually lose their power. By contrast, the stepparent who acquires responsibility for stepchildren in a remarriage after divorce must come to terms with the continued existence of the parent who has been replaced and whose sometimes unexpected and unpredictable interventions may continue to shape the fabric of everyday life in the new family.

There is a variety of evidence suggesting that many non-custodial parents gradually lose contact with children by a first marriage (Eekelaar and Clive, 1977; Maidment, 1975; Masson and Burgoyne, 1979; Murch, 1980). From the accounts of the non-custodial parents in our own sample it is not difficult to see why this happens so frequently. Fathers who, during first marriage, had played a relatively inactive part in the day-to-day care of their young children found it especially difficult to sustain any relationship with their children after they had separated; they frequently had nowhere to entertain their children and were unsure how best to spend their time with them. Other difficulties occur later; visits to a former wife's home might become difficult and embarrassing when she acquires a new partner and as children grow older they often develop friendships and interests which disrupt earlier patterns of access. The payment of maintenance and the exercise of access therefore tend to be linked, so that if a father is unwilling or unable to pay maintenance he feels unable to exercise his rights of access. Conversely, if he is unable to see his children he feels under less obligation to pay maintenance. Many of the mothers we studied were also willing to forego maintenance if it meant that they were no longer inconvenienced by visits from their ex-partner. This attitude was especially prevalent after remarriage, when their children had acquired a stepfather who, it was felt, now provided the main source of financial stability in the family, so that contact with the non-custodial father no longer merited the social costs involved. Consequently, although part of the orthodoxy which provides a foundation for contemporary legal and social work practice advocates active and spontaneous contacts between non-custodial parents and their children, this appears, from our evidence, rarely to be translated into practice by those involved. This disparity between the ideals of public policy and the realities of post-divorce behaviour raises important questions about the origins of values and beliefs attached to parenthood in our society.

When we go on to examine the process of family reconstitution itself and compare the experiences of stepmothers and stepfathers, differences in male and female role obligations emerge very clearly and are themselves illustrative of more widely acknowledged gender differences in the meanings and relative importance of the parental role for men and women. Through an examination of the meaning of *step*motherhood and *step*fatherhood it may therefore be possible to gain a new perspective on motherhood and fatherhood in general.

Becoming a Stepmother

As the Newsons have suggested, what constitutes a good mother in our society is more closely and clearly defined than what constitutes being a good father. A mother's role obligations are held to be at once both more specific and more encompassing than those of the father. Such expectations therefore promote a division of labour in which mothers not only bear chief responsibility for everyday care and maintenance but also for how children behave or "turn out" in the long term. When their sample were aged four, the Newsons concluded:

> "Fathers are not expected to take public responsibility for either the behaviour or the appearance of young children and blame will be transferred to the mother even where father has voluntarily accepted the major involvement." (Newson and Newson, 1968)

At the age of seven they found that,

> ". . . the main burden of maintenance of discipline at this age rests firmly upon the mother." (Newson and Newson, 1976)

Consequently, and notwithstanding an increasing general interest in the father's role, women with little previous experience of children who become stepmothers face a much harder task than their male counterparts. They will usually be expected to take on the many domestic duties of daily childcare and will also become accountable in public as the principal custodians of their acquired children. It is thus a much bigger step towards family reconstitution and the recreation of "normal" family life when a formerly motherless family acquires a stepmother than when a stepfather joins a female single-parent household, and for both children and father her arrival signals the resumption of a more normal family life. George and Wilding's (1972) study of motherless families clearly demonstrated the extent of lone fathers' reliance on outside domestic help from kin, paid employees and public agencies. New partners of custodian fathers therefore often appear as an immediate solution to pressing domestic problems and feel themselves to be welcomed or judged in those terms. In such situations, different aspects of female ideals and expectations may be in conflict. Contemporary ideologies of romantic love and marital partnership stress the centrality of an intimate relationship which is chosen for itself and which is expected to become a major preoccupation, at least during the early stages of marriage. However, women are also expected and encouraged to imagine themselves as mothers and to anticipate the fulfilment which it is believed motherhood will embody. Thus a single woman who falls in love and plans to marry a father with custody of children may be expected to respond readily to the opportunity of becoming an "instant" parent. Consequently, many stepmothers begin their new partnerships with idealized expectations of their capacity to restore and recreate a satisfying domestic life for their new family (see, for example Maddox, 1975). However, those who have never had children of their own will find inevitable "gaps" in their experience which greatly affect their evaluation of their own performance as mothers. In our study we found that the previously childless stepmothers were particularly anxious to stress those aspects of their lives which demonstrated their familiarity with and fondness for children. In addition they were eager to have children of their own and all but one of them had done so. As a result, they were able to use their subsequent experiences of having children both to confirm their authenticity as mothers and to make sense of any difficulties they had with their stepchildren. It may, therefore, be particularly important for previously childless stepmothers to have a child of their own in their new marriage.

Those stepmothers in our study who had acquired their stepchildren when they were still very young had found this reassuring. Generally, they believed that the younger the children were when they first knew them, the more they were able to mould or influence them, ameliorating the adverse effects of the inevitable changes which took place when their parents split up. It was clear that in such circumstances stepmothers found it easier to become "real" mothers than those whose stepchildren were older when the new family was formed and for whom many of the usual problems of adolescence might be compounded by the steprelationship.

The stepmothers we interviewed showed great awareness of their responsibility and accountability for their stepchildren's health, development and general progress. In particular, they frequently referred to ways in which children had improved and "settled down" since their arrival, drawing, where necessary, on the opinions and evaluations of kin, teachers and others who had known the children before they had acquired a stepmother. Their accounts included references to the children's physical and emotional well-being, especially getting on better at school and making friends more easily, as well as to those more mundane matters which make up the warp and woof of family life; enjoying meals, family expeditions and leisure-time, sharing in household tasks, and having their stepchildren well turned out. In this sense, stepmothers are essential to the reconstitu-tion of ordinary family life for motherless families in a way not shared by their male counterparts.

Becoming a Stepfather

It was evident from their replies to our questions about their step-children and current family circumstances, that the stepfathers in our study saw their stepparental obligations chiefly in terms of the material and emotional support they could offer the children's mother. They frequently contrasted their wives' recollections of the difficult and lonely period of single parenthood which they had gone through before they met, with their present happiness, stability and greater economic security as a family. Their accounts illustrate clearly the extent to which the family responsibilities of fathers are frequently seen as indirectly, though supportively, related to those of their wives, whose domestic and emotional commitment remains the indispensable foundation for "normal" family life. Consequently, many stepfathers emphasized improvements in their wives' and stepchildren's material circumstances, ways in which their standard of living had improved or simply the greater economic security their wives had gained through remarriage. In addition, they were pleased to demonstrate how their presence had recreated a partnership and normal family life for their wives, thus enabling them to face public encounters with schools, welfare agencies and so on, with greater equanimity. It was also important for them to feel that they offered basic support to their wives in relation to the management and discipline of children. Additionally, many stepfathers mentioned traditionally "male" interests and skills which they contributed to the family group, believing that a wide range of domestic tasks was best accomplished by a "man in the house".

Like the stepmothers, the stepfathers in our study felt they had been able to have more influence on their stepchildren when the children had still been very young at the time of remarriage, but it is evident that many viewed their contribution to the upbringing of children in more indirect, even impersonal, terms, so that whilst bachelors and those who had previously been childless may have been unused to the demands of dependent children, they did not usually feel that it was necessary to compensate for their formerly childless status in the same way as the stepmothers. Male parental responsibilities were therefore seen chiefly in terms of supporting their wives and in the everyday circumstances of family finances and organization — such matters as being able to provide the dinner money, mend a puncture, or ferry children in the car. Where such duties were seen to make up the constituent elements of fatherhood, then it was difficult for some men to see how they could go on being a "real" father to their children by a former marriage when, for example, their visits were infrequent and tightly structured. This became even more difficult in those cases where non-custodial children had gone on to acquire a new stepfather of their own who had taken on such responsibilities.

Stepparents therefore typically visualize and act out their role obligations in terms of both their *actual* experiences of parenthood and against a backcloth of generalized public expectations. The private experience of parenting is thus extremely vulnerable to images, constraints and ideologies which are generated in more public arenas. This tension between public and private is further illustrated when we consider the decision to have a baby in a remarriage.

Childbearing in Remarriage

When we consider the circumstances which may surround the decision to have a subsequent child in a remarriage it is soon apparent that many of the assumptions, rules-of-thumb and commonsense knowledge and skills which attend parenthood in unbroken families become more explicit and take on a different significance the second time around. This is revealed most tellingly in the manner in which the remarried are continually confronted by an emotional and material inheritance from the past which continues to influence, shape and constrain future behaviour and aspirations. Accordingly, individual theories and rationalizations about first marriage and the reasons for divorce may combine to set important guidelines in a remarriage. Our study has shown, for example, that an individual's explanation of marriage break-down, and the subjective meanings which he or she attaches to it, may be of considerable importance in shaping subsequent experiences. So too, in thinking about having another child, a variety of factors may present themselves for consideration which would not be relevant to a couple having a baby in a first marriage but which are nevertheless increasingly relevant to our total understanding of child-bearing in different contexts. By definition, the couples we studied were already a family, since one or other partner had brought a child or children from a previous marriage; their decisions about further child-bearing thus drew upon different aspects of belief about the nature of parenthood as well as their own earlier experience of parental responsibility. They displayed, therefore, a conscious application to the process of reconstituting family life out of the diversity of past experiences.

A number of considerations may combine to encourage or inhibit reproduction in a stepfamily. In most cases the major determinants derive from the persisting legacy of previous marriage. The most commonly cited, if pragmatic, reason for having another baby in a remarriage, especially in a step sibling family where both partners have retained custody of children, is the sense of unity which it is believed such a child will confer. Couples speak of the way in which having another child has created a "bond" or "seal" in the family, thereby "bringing everyone together" as one unit. A frequently-used illustration of this is found in the alleged subjugation of stepsibling rivalries in the face of common affection for a new baby. More diffusely articulated is the desire, felt by some couples, to have a child together as an expression of the love-relationship existing between them and a confirmation of their partnership. For parents and stepchildren alike such a child might serve, in origin and name, as a symbol of the family's new collective identity. Certainly there are senses in which children are regarded not only as the bricks which make up the family structure but also the foundations upon which its future achievements will rest. Parents see in their children both image and extension of themselves as well as a potential source of new accomplishments. Having another child might therefore serve as an outlet for these beliefs and help to "normalize" patterns of family development in the future.

On the other hand, a number of circumstances and constraints may militate against having more children. These might be biographical or structural, or more likely both. In some cases age might be a primary reason. Older couples who remarry, if not actually infertile, may feel that having babies is an aspect of the personal life-cycle which for them is completed and not to be resumed. Indeed, in some cases, remarried couples actively look forward to the departure of their teenage children in eager anticipation of the autonomy and personal freedom which they believe will ensue. Others feel that another child might create an imbalance of the age structure within the family, with an inordinate age-gap between the youngest child and its half siblings. The extent to which this was perceived as a problem among the couples we studied was usually related to the family's overall self-image and the degree to which its members were concerned with either masking or laying bare those salient aspects of the family's history concerning divorce and remarriage.

For some couples, decisions about more children may be tempered by perceptions of marriage break-up and the role of children within it. For example, those men who feel that neglect of their children, perhaps because of involvement in work, was a contributory factor in the break-up of a former marriage, might be loath to have another child in case such pressures should arise again. In cases where one partner is previously unmarried differing horizons of expectation are likely to ensue. This is perhaps most graphically illustrated in those situations where the remarrying partner has undergone sterilization during former marriage.

Other constraints may be more overtly material and economic. The stepfamily, typically, will be on average larger than its unbroken counterpart. There may therefore be difficulties in obtaining adequate accommodation, which can be further complicated by issues arising out of financial settlement at divorce. Payment and receipt of maintenance can also create financial barriers to having another child in a situation where the stability of the family budget is dependent upon the regular receipt of maintenance payments. "Chains" of such payments are not uncommon and can interlock the financial circumstances of a number of otherwise unconnected families, with possible long-term effects on their development. However, being able to "afford" another child may not only be a fiscal matter; it may also be determined by the adequacy of legal arrangements made at the time of divorce. Thus where patterns of custody and access are subject to changes resulting from continuing legal conflict, then a couple might feel that to have another child would be injudicious and likely to cause further disruption to family life.

Decisions about further child-bearing in a stepfamily are therefore likely to be surrounded by a number of conflicting judgements and evaluations. Insofar as couples who remarry do consider having another child, however, they are likely to do so sooner, rather than later. In contrast to their once-married counterparts, separated or divorced parents are likely to have second courtships which are themselves heavily tinged with parental and domestic obligations and in which children may play a central part (Burgoyne and Clark, 1980 p. 14). Accordingly, even before formal remarriage takes place, and as we have seen it is frequently preceded by cohabitation, there may well have been some discussions about having another child. Unlike most men and women who marry for the first time, stepparents and their partners already have responsibility for the day-to-day care and control of children and are consequently denied that period of being alone together, and establishing an identity as a couple, which is often so important in first marriage. The remarrying are therefore likely to develop new approaches to parenting in a situation where pre-existing limits and constraints are set upon the subsequent development of family life.

Conclusions

In conclusion, we would like to draw attention to some of the wider implications of our work on stepparents and their children. As our research has progressed we have become increasingly aware of the dangers of ascribing too great an importance to the *step*family as a determinant of all that happens within families in which parents remarry. In many respects, the experiences of the parents and stepparents we studied seem remarkably similar to those of parents in first marriages. In making sense of this we have, of course, been bedevilled by the lack of comparative data on ordinary families. Nevertheless, it often seemed to be the case that the couples we spoke to were inclined to interpret their family experiences in terms of beliefs about the long-term consequences for children of divorce and remarriage. This frequently presented them with an explanatory framework wherein *all* problematic aspects of a child's behaviour could be given some meaning. There was a tendency to view the typical problems of, for example, dealing with adolescent children, the like of which might have been common in any similarly situated unbroken family, as difficulties arising out of the legacy of divorce. As sociologists we have thus found it necessary to remind ourselves that the extent to which stepfamilies differ from other family types and from each other, is frequently related to social class and subcultural variations and to location within the family life-cycle, as much as to any intrinsic characteristics which they may have as a product of divorce and remarriage. For example, the poorest families in our study have more in common with other families experiencing poverty and can be better understood in relation to data on poverty. Likewise the self-ascribed "civilized" attitudes towards divorce, remarriage and steprelationships expressed by some of the middle class couples make more sense when seen in terms of the dominant, bourgeois culture of which they are a part. Above all else, however, and this is at the heart of our problem here, it is because divorce and remarriage is frequently an *attempt* to reconstitute family life along apparently "normal" lines, that we are able to see mirrored in the family lives of the remarried some of the prevailing concerns of all families of their particular class, culture or community. The extent to which it is possible to recreate the normal in this way is determined however by a variety of personal and structural constraints which we have portrayed as the legacy of divorce.

Where the issue is parent–child relationships, then it is possible to show how idealized conceptions of "normal" family life, on the one hand, and the actual experience of family reconstitution, on the other, may come into abrasive contact. It is clear that both parties in a re-marriage will have differing past experiences concerning child-bearing and -rearing and will take on new and perhaps unfamiliar obligations and duties. For example, single parents are able to relinquish sole responsibility for their offspring, non-custodial parents will acquire "new" children and non-parents will have their first taste of parenthood, albeit in different circumstances from those of a natural parent. The stepfamily thus presents an interesting juxtaposition between what we might call "blood" and "social" parenting. These might be distinguished in terms of the way in which parenthood is felt to fulfil certain needs. On the one hand, having a child or children may be related to beliefs about the significance of blood ties. For example, it might be considered important to reproduce something of oneself to pass into the future or felt that to mingle one's own genetic inheritance with that of a loved partner is to create the unique product of a particular relationship. So too, "giving birth" or "fathering" a child may be an experience containing deep biological and psychological fulfilment. On the other hand, it is possible to emphasize the *social* aspects of parenting as a worthwhile, pleasurable and desirable set of activities. Parenting in this sense might mean such things as the confirmation of adult status, along with responsibility for daily events which are felt to be intrinsically satisfying. Children might also be regarded as a source of future investment, providing a family with continuity and stability.

If we consider this distinction within the context of the stepfamily, then it is apparent that those felt needs which centre around the idea of blood-parenting cannot be fulfilled by the stepparental relationship alone. The social dimension of parenting, however, may be similarly perceived by step- and natural parent alike. Exploration of the relative importance attached to the new dimensions may therefore serve as a way of examining the meaning of parenthood in a variety of settings; for example, the distinction could also be applied to foster and adoptive parents.

In the stepfamily the relative dominance of "blood" and "social" factors may have important consequences at various levels, such as day-to-day family organization and routine, feelings about the appropriateness of the family's structure and image, and, of course, attitudes towards further child-bearing. Thus for those men and women who identify the social as the paramount dimension of their stepparental role, the duties and tasks which go with it will constitute an adequate basis for thinking about themselves as parents. For those who see the blood component as a *sine qua non* of total parenting, there is likely to be a strong desire to go on to have another child. In either case there will be certain constraints placed upon the development of family life which differ from those in unbroken families but which nevertheless allow us to use the variant in order to throw light on the normal.

Acknowledgements

The research upon which this paper is based was funded initially by the Sheffield City Polytechnic and latterly by the Social Science Research Council. The support of both organizations is gratefully acknowledged.

References

Burgoyne, J. and Clark, D. (1980). Why get married again? *New Society*, **52**, No. 913, 12–14.

Busfield, J. (1974). Ideologies and reproduction. In *The Integration of a Child into a Social World*. Edited by M. P. M. Richards. Cambridge: Cambridge University Press.

Chester, R. (1971). The duration of marriage to divorce. *British Journal of Sociology*, **22**, 172–182.

Dunnell, K. (1979). *Family Formation 1976*. OPCS Report SS 1080. London: HMSO.

Eekelaar, J. and Clive, E. (1977). *Custody After Divorce*. Oxford: SSRC Centre for Socio-Legal Studies.

George, V. and Wilding, P. (1972). *Motherless Families*. London: Routledge and Kegan Paul.

Leete, R. (1979). *Changing Patterns of Family Formation and Dissolution in England and Wales 1964–75*. Studies on Medical and Population Subjects, No. 39. London: HMSO.

Macintyre, S. (1976). Who wants babies? The social construction of "instincts". In *Sexual Divisions and Society*. Edited by D. L. Barker and S. Allen. London: Tavistock Publications.

Maddox, B. (1975). *The Half Parent*. London: Andre Deutsch.

Maidment, S. (1975). Access conditions in custody orders. *British Journal of Law and Society*, **2**, 182–200.

Marsden, D. (1973). *Mothers Alone: Poverty and the Fatherless Family*. Harmondsworth, Middlesex: Penguin Books.

Masson, J. and Burgoyne, J. (1979). *The English Stepfamily*. Paper presented at the Third World Conference of the International Society of Family Law, Uppsala, June, 1979.

Murch, M. (1980). *Justice and Welfare in Divorce*. London: Sweet and Maxwell.

Newson, J. and Newson, E. (1968). *Four Years Old in an Urban Community*. London: Allen and Unwin.

Newson, J. and Newson, E. (1976). *Seven Years Old in the Home Environment*. Harmondsworth, Middlesex: Pelican Books.

Rapoport, R. and Rapoport, R. N. (1981). *Families in Britain*. London: Routledge and Kegan Paul.

Rapoport, R., Rapoport, R. N. and Strelitz, Z. (1977). *Fathers, Mothers and Others: Towards New Alliances*. London: Routledge and Kegan Paul.

Thornes, B. and Collard, J. (1979). *Who Divorces?* London: Routledge and Kegan Paul.

Child Rearing
by Lone Fathers

TONY HIPGRAVE

School of Social Work,
University of Leicester, Leicester, England

"Father do the best he can when the mother is gone
Father do the best he can when the mother is gone
Father do the best he can
But there's so many things he just don't understand
Motherless children have a hard time when their mother is gone".
(from "Motherless Children", traditional American Folk song).

Introduction

In 1978 there were an estimated 825,000 single-parent families in Great Britain, caring for some 1,250,000 children (Hansard, 1980a). Some 100,000 of these families were headed by a lone father, involving around 180,000 children. Assuming a growth rate of 6% per annum, as was the case between 1971 and 1976 (Leete, 1978) — and the ever-rising divorce rate would appear to support the assumption — a conservative estimate would place the number of single-parent families in 1980 at 925,000 and the number of children concerned at around 1½ million. Of these, 115,000 families and 200,000 children may well fall within the scope of this paper on child-rearing by lone fathers.

What I hope to demonstrate in this paper is that although we have very little evidence that lone fathers are not perfectly capable of raising well-adjusted children, it is nonetheless possible to identify factors which can make lone fatherhood problematic for both father and child. ionally, points are illustrated by quotations which come from an tudy of a group of 16 lone fathers which I conducted in 1978 78).

149

Fatherhood

Recent years have witnessed a substantial erosion of the assumption that fathers play at best a minimal role in the upbringing of their children. The necessarily pivotal nature of the mother–child relationship has been called into question from a number of directions, notably (i) analyses of mothering as a continuing series of activities and attitudes not necessarily biologically pre-determined (e.g. Schaffer, 1977); (ii) survey findings that fathers are in fact often very involved in a practical sense in the upbringing of their children (e.g. Newson and Newson, 1963, 1968); and (iii) research on the phenomenon of infant attachments which reveals that attachment is not necessarily, as Bowlby claimed, "monotropic" (Bowlby, 1953) but may apply to more than one individual, and that attachments, which may differ qualitatively between individuals, are not necessarily predictable by how much time the individual spends with the infant or by specific activities, such as feeding (Ainsworth, 1979).

To argue for the indispensability of either parent in a general sense would be presumptuous and foolhardy, both because the contribution of parents can never be truly independent and because families do not happen to work in conveniently dyadic ways. Families are units in a constant state of negotiation, both internally and with the external world, both on an individual plane and collectively.

Lone Fatherhood

DEFINITIONAL PROBLEMS

For the purposes of this paper we may define a lone father as a man having sole responsibility for the day-to-day parenting of his children. This definition includes, for example, cases where the children see their mother from time to time but excludes cases where the father has a regular cohabitee or lives with his parents.

Becoming a single parent involves a double adjustment for men. It means both becoming single (see Hetherington *et al.*, 1976) and becoming the major parent, a combination which for men does no admit of any readily available social role or status. The circumstanc by which a man becomes a single parent will also vary enormou These encompass death of a spouse, separation, divorce and being left with a child though unmarried. These last three m an atmosphere of hostility or mutuality and the father ma keep his children or simply have been left with them. Further compounding factors include the age, sex and number of children, the father's employment, the nature of any continuing relationship with a spouse or ex-spouse, and the ready availability of support. One American study identified at least nine different types of single parent status, allowing for remarriages (Greenberg, 1979).

In practice, 48% of lone fathers in Great Britain are caring for one child, 32% for two children and 20% for three or more children. More than 80% of lone fathers are likely to be over thirty-five and 90% of the children concerned over five years of age (Leete, 1978; *OPCS Monitor*, 1978). In the National Children's Bureau Study (Ferri, 1976; Ferri and Robinson, 1976) motherless families were equally divided between those caused by death and those by divorce or separation, while unmarried lone fathers were a rarity. The division for fatherless families is approximately ¼ widowed, ⅕ single unmarried and just over ½ divorced/separated (Office of Population Censuses and Surveys, 1978). Motherless families tend to contain more boys (63% of children) than girls (37%), unlike fatherless families (45% and 55% respectively) (Ferri, 1976).

Just how different the position of widowers and divorced or separated husbands might be is difficult to assess. Certainly one would assume that the position of the widower is in many ways a more "acceptable" one, in that it is less likely to involve a large-scale disruption of previous friendships and other relationships. Equally one may assume that the absence of an interested, and possibly hostile, parental party might lead to a less complex overall emotional environment for parent and child; this is borne out by studies which have compared the later adjustment of children from widowed and divorced families (e.g. Douglas *et al.*, 1968; Douglas, 1970; Rutter, 1972). On the other hand the re-negotiation of the parent–child relationship, with its potential pressures of time, feelings and money, has similar elements for both widowed and divorced/separated groups. Furthermore, the wife and mother is not completely absent from the widowed family's life. A sort of negotiation *in absentia* occurs, possibly healthy or unhealthy, and possibly including elements similar to those described in clinical work with families created by marital breakdown (see Gardner, 1976, for a review of this area). Some writers, notably Marris (1974), have suggested that the dynamics of the wider concepts w...ss and change may be useful in understanding similarities between Occas:ement and divorce.

in-depth ser the similarities and differences might be between lone (Hipgrave, 1 casioned by death and marital breakdown, there is little doubt that the latter phenomenon can take a far greater variety of courses. Mendes (1976a) has grouped lone fathers by marital breakdown into *assenters* and *seekers*, the former effectively being left with children, the latter actively seeking custody. Each group can exist in an atmosphere of *aggression* or *conciliation*. Mendes' model thus offers four ways of becoming a lone father: aggressive seeking, conciliatory seeking, aggressive initiation by the other spouse or conciliatory initiation by the other spouse. O'Brien (1980) suggests that the important point is less the decision to parent as such, than the style in which the transition to single parenthood is negotiated. In her sample it was working-class families who tended to display more aggression during this transition whilst middle-class families tended more towards a conciliatory model.

In recent years as divorce has been conceptualized not as an event but as a sequence of experiences for all parties, there has been a general move amongst probation and other welfare services towards divorce experience courses and other means of bringing parties to a conciliatory solution in order to minimize the negative and potentially lingering effects of fighting custody (see e.g. Fraser, 1980). Nonetheless, as Hetherington *et al.* (1979) have repeatedly pointed out in their series of studies on divorce, there can simply be no such thing as a "victimless" divorce.

Detailed statistics are not kept in a form which addresses the issue of which parent is more likely to obtain custody. In 90 per cent of custody cases the children go to their mother; on the other hand, only six per cent of cases are defended. In 99 per cent of uncontested cases and 95 per cent of contested cases, the residential status quo is upheld. Thus if a father keeps his children after separation and later contests custody, his chances of obtaining custody appear to be statistically good. If, however, a mother chooses to appeal against a paternal custody order the chances are much greater that the residential *status quo* will be overturned than if a father appeals against an order in favour of the mother (Maidment, 1980). These statistics seem to support in part both the liberal position that the child should go to the "psychological parent" and that the "least detrimental of any available alternatives for the child" should be the major criterion for decision (Goldstein *et al.*, 1974), and, to a lesser degree, the accusation that judges do tend to have a slight bias against awarding custody to fathers. The Finer Report (Finer, 1974) and a number of pressure groups have suggested that a less formal and legalistic system, involving a panel of professionals outside the legal profession, should be introduced to ensure that decisions are taken on a psychologically informed basis and that hostilities between parties are kept to a minimum.

Separated, but not divorced, lone fathers may suffer additional difficulties to do with the temporal uncertainty of their position. This can lead to a complex series of peaks and troughs of external and internal pressures (Chiriboga and Cutler, 1977).

RESEARCH

There have been a number of studies of lone fatherhood in the last decade. Such studies have been conducted in a number of countries including Australia (Bain, 1973), Canada (Todres, 1975), the U.S.A. (Mendes, 1975b; Orthner *et al.*, 1976; Gasser and Taylor, 1976; Keshet and Rosenthal, 1978a, 1978b; Levine, 1976) and Great Britain (Hipgrave, 1978; O'Brien, 1978). There have been surveys of motherless families designed to extract common characteristics of such families (George and Wilding, 1972; Ferri, 1973). There have also been books and articles describing personal experiences of lone parenthood, both fathers' and mothers' (e.g. Barber, 1975); offering practical advice to lone parents of either sex (e.g. Davenport, 1979; Brown, 1980); and describing social work intervention with lone fathers (Murch, 1973).

For a number of reasons we should be cautious about comparing data between studies. In his review of the literature on motherless families, however, Schlesinger (1978) identifies a number of common themes: (1) financial problems; (2) child care problems — mainly to do with obtaining help or relief; (3) problems to do with the father's own personal life; (4) homemaking and housework difficulties; (5) personal stress; (6) problems to do with relating to the community at large. More succinctly, George and Wilding (1972) assert that there are problems of *time*, of *money* and of *feelings*.

Time: Problems to do with time can take many forms. On one level they are connected with the decision to carry on working — which most lone fathers do (roughly five out of six — Hansard, 1980b) — or not. The problem of combining employment with homemaking and parenting is a common one for all lone parents, and free social time as a family is scarce. School holidays are particularly bad times for working lone parents, who have to seek out day-care provision for their children (George and Wilding, 1972; Hipgrave, 1978), and another major series of recommendations by the Finer Committee (Finer, 1974), like the majority of its recommendations still awaiting implementation, concerned the need for more flexible working arrangements for single parents and vastly improved day-care facilities.

Thus for working lone parents the "time" problem can consist of having too little time for the pleasanter aspects of parenting or personal pursuits, and constantly attempting to allocate time and resources in the best interests of the children. Although the majority of lone fathers do continue working, some 35% of George and Wilding's (1972) sample had been forced to give up work at some point to care for their children full-time. Some had returned to work, but there is a significant minority of lone parents who become full-time parents to their children. (The American studies do not seem ever to include a group of such fathers.)

For many men work is, in a way, part of their social life and for many lone fathers work is a crucial social outlet from the sometimes claustrophobic pursuits of single parenthood. Those fathers who choose to give up work consciously renounce this often unappreciated aspect of work life, and often find that time weighs heavily upon them. By reducing their family income — sometimes drastically — giving up work reduces leisure options, at least those which cost money. It can also provide too much time for fathers to contemplate their desolation, or appreciate their isolation.

The decision whether or not to give up work can be an extremely stressful one for lone fathers, a decision usually made at a time of numerous other personal and practical pressures. To make the decision involves the acceptance of inevitable negative consequences both for the father and his family. One full-time father explained his immediate major reaction to his wife's departure thus:

"I was worried about packing up work. Funny you know, that was all I was worried about. I tried to get her back for a week, but I think it was only because I wanted to go back to work. I don't think I wanted *her* back at all".

Another full-time lone father put his major problem thus:

"You've got time on your hands, but it's not usable time, you can't do anything with it. You've got time on your hands but you haven't".

Most full-time fathers go through periods of lethargy and extreme aggressive frustration at the feeling of being trapped at home, especially in the first few months after giving up work. A consciously-taken decision to leave work can sometimes have devastating and unforeseen consequences for the full-time father and his health, at least in the short-term. In such circumstances men are not generally socialized into asking for help and thus many lone fathers endure a considerable amount of anger and depression until they adjust their life-style satisfactorily.

Money: Problems to do with money can concern either the family income or how it is managed. George and Wilding (1972) found that in 44% of their motherless families the family income had decreased as a result of the family's new status. Only 12% of these cases could be accounted for by loss of a wife's earnings. Thus, if their study is of general application George and Wilding's findings would indicate that one-third of motherless families have a drop in income attributable to the father's earning less money. At one extreme, this may involve having to live on social security. For householders with a mortgage this can mean having to sell the house and move into rented accommodation, as social security repayments do not generally cover mortgage repayments adequately. For fathers still in employment, overtime may be limited for the sake of the family, or a new and more convenient job found. Whatever the reason for a drop in income, its effect will be not only to reduce a family's material standards but also to limit the number and nature of activities open to them. Ferri (1976), too, found that all groups of single parents in the National Children's Bureau study suffered material disadvantage and a drop in their standard of living. Whether or not there is an actual drop in income, a proportion of fathers have difficulties — at least initially — in managing the household budget. For most this is merely a new learning task and is dealt with in this way but for men who have never had to shop wisely, or to place priorities on purchases, money-management can be yet another headache.

Feelings: There are probably as many combinations of problems broadly to do with "feelings" as there are individual lone fathers, and once again we can only suggest common themes, which may or may not be applicable to individual cases. The general context of these psychological factors is a series of fundamental conflicts, notably between the demands of the past and the future, and between the needs of the father and those of his children. Broadly speaking, stresses involving the time and money aspects already mentioned can be compounded by any of the following:

(i) *Feelings related to the reactions of others.* "The figure of the deserted male left to look after children is one that attracts sympathetic assistance from every quarter" (Sanctuary and Whitehead, 1970). It is open to question whether this claim is wholly accurate. On the one hand Ferri (1976) found that far more lone fathers than lone mothers had the ready assistance of a fellow care-taker of the opposite sex (24% and 5% respectively). On the other hand, as has already been suggested, men are not socialized into asking for personal assistance, except perhaps in dire straits.

Mendes (1976a) noted a paradox amongst her sample of American lone fathers, concerning the different uses of helping resources between assenting and seeking fathers:

"As a group, the assenters appeared to need social services the most; ironically, however, they were least likely to seek out or utilize such resources. Because they generally had greater motivation to succeed as single parents, seekers made use of more social services and other resources than did assenters."

Certainly there appears from the various interview studies to be no shortage of sympathetic reaction to the lone father's situation, but sympathy divorced from the assistance which is needed—if not actually asked for—can often have a negative effect on lone fathers, who feel in need of reassurance as to their competence as parents. This is because sympathy can sometimes unwittingly stem from a belief that by breaking one of society's developmental codes—namely that an intact family unit is the ideal mode of rearing children—lone fathers are doomed to personal difficulties and their children to developmental harm. This is illustrated in the following quotation:

"A lot of people are sympathetic but I'm not too struck on them being too sympathetic. A bit of sympathy's alright, it boosts your ego a bit, but if they come out and say 'You're coping very well but it is a pity', it sort of clashes, doesn't it? You're saying the opposite to what you mean."

(ii) *Feelings of loneliness.* This group of feelings can involve at least three components. Firstly, it is linked to the availability of support systems, which for the vast majority of lone fathers studied so far denotes informal systems, notably the father's own family. Secondly, many lone fathers have met very few, if any, men, in a similar position to themselves. Some may do so via single parents' groups, notably Gingerbread, but such groups attract by no means the majority of lone parents in a particular area. Exceptionally, attempts have been made to bring together motherless families on a social or therapeutic basis (Brown and Stones, 1979). Thirdly, there is the issue of personal intimacy with other adults, summarized in the simple quotation below:

"You know your kids love you, but it's a different sort of love, you know. I suppose I feel as though I want to be wanted."

A recent American study (Greenberg, 1979) has sought to highlight differences in this area of adjustment between lone fathers and lone mothers. Whilst both groups felt that personal autonomy was the major benefit of single parenthood, both groups experienced problems of sexual adjustment, being caught in a sexual no man's land between the freedom of a single "swinger" and the comforts of marital sex. Fathers seemed to be allowed more behavioural latitude in this area than mothers, but discomfort from *loneliness* was almost exclusively limited to lone fathers. The less liberal sexual scripts offered to women seemed more than counterbalanced by a strong same-sex friendship network, denied to men, which made for greater leisure-role satisfactions and thus appeared to allow single mothers greater appreciation of the benefits of independence gained by being single again. Intimacy, in the sense of intimate relationships, may be an important factor militating against the onset of depressive reactions (Brown and Harris, 1978).

With male friends, lone fathers often find that their personal priorities have shifted in a way which makes relationships less reciprocal. Informal, non-sexual relationships with females outside the father's own family are difficult. One father put his dilemma this way.

"I think I'm distrusted. I don't know whether it's me subconsciously thinking this way, you know. I don't like going in a woman's house if her husband's not there. It took me ages to go in next door, till she said 'don't worry, he'll not think you're knocking me off — he knows me better than that. It doesn't matter what the neighbours think'."

Whether this neighbourhood gossip genuinely exists, or merely represents the father's perceptions of others' reactions, this real or imaginary attitude limits the interactions of many lone fathers, particularly full-time fathers. When lone fathers do establish intimate relationships with a member of the opposite sex, in addition to the problem of how the woman friend and children interact, the role, or potential role, of the friend in the household causes fathers some concern, as they have perforce taken over many of their former partner's practical functions. A lone father of seven years standing with four children graphically described how this problem operated for him:

"When you've got the opportunity of having a relationship with another bird, you can't really say, 'Here you are you do that job' — a job that the wife was doing — and then you revert to your old job, because you're so conditioned to doing things yourself. You become that critical that you often ruin your relationship with the bird."

Particularly in the first few months of lone fatherhood, many men are often swinging wildly between their need to ease their feelings of desolation, and to provide for their children's needs. This can cause the lone father considerable personal confusion:

> "You're very isolated and it's a vicious circle because you stay in to look after the kids, and so naturally you lose a lot of friends, therefore you become more isolated. I felt there was this conflict there between my nature as a person — the desire for a sexual and social life — and my relationship with the kids."

(iii) *Feelings to do with manhood:* This group of feelings can also involve a number of elements (see e.g. Fasteau, 1976). For those fathers who have to give up work, in a society where to be an economic provider is still one of the major components of manhood, this can lead to feelings of being, to quote one father, "a second class person". In a random street survey, George and Wilding (1972) found that 86% of those questioned considered that single parent mothers should stay at home to care for their children, but a staggering 78% felt that fathers in the same position should go out to work rather than become house-husbands. Full-time fathers consistently report being regularly confronted with this attitude, not least from professionals operating in welfare and social security agencies.

A further element in this group of feelings concerns public tasks which the father finds himself having to perform, which are usually the preserve of a mother:

> "You feel a bit — er — you get one or two queer looks. You notice it especially when you're looking through kiddies' pants and things like that. There you are looking through kiddies' pants and they're thinking 'Ey up, we've got a right one here.' You can see it, you can feel them looking at you."

Once again, whether these attitudes are real or imaginary, for the lone father his perceptions are the only reality which matters, and for him this involves a questioning of his own sexual identity by others.

(iv) *Feelings to do with competence as a parent.* The intensity of these sorts of feelings is related inevitably to the age and sex of any children concerned, the nature of the father's previous parenting role (and it is worth recalling that the evidence is that it is a minority of men who will be totally naive in care-taking activities) and, to a lesser extent, the continuing role of the former spouse.

There is no reason to suppose that lone fathers themselves should be immune from the prevailing assumptions that the mother is the more important parent, particularly of younger children, and that a two-parent family is the "proper" environment for the healthy development of children. Mendes (1979) calls this "the tyranny of the two-parent model".

Three common elements in popular assumptions about parenthood often affect the sensitivity of a number of lone fathers particularly strongly. Firstly, there is what one might call the "volcano effect". This states that although most children might, surprisingly, not show acute signs of distress after the death or disappearance of their mother (Marris, 1958; Marsden, 1969; George and Wilding, 1972), and though to all appearances a child may appear well-adjusted, being brought up in a one-parent family *per se* involves stresses, which simmer slowly and are bound to erupt at some later point in the child's development.

A widower with a young daughter expressed this as follows:

"Yes, I've got a certain sense of pride, in that things seem to have gone OK. People are always complimenting you on how well she's behaved and all the rest of it. I don't think much about that because you're always waiting for the next kick in the face. I don't know whether it will all sort of pop out when she's 14 or 15 or whether she is genuinely growing up adjusted."

Secondly, feelings of parental inadequacy are usually less concerned with the tasks involved in child-care than potential emotional deficits, in particular children's needs for what in common parlance is termed "mother love". Many lone fathers — even those aware and convinced of their own general competence — feel that as men they are inevitably depriving their children emotionally, as illustrated below:

"I know I can't give them motherly love. That's the one thing. I can be everything, but I can't be a mother to them."

Thirdly, there is the issue of whether men can adequately parent girls. There is in fact little evidence either for or against the popular assumption (reflected, as has already been noted, in the actual statistical make-up of single parent families) that parenting daughters is more problematic for lone fathers than lone mothers (Santrock and Warshak, 1979). Much more evidence exists on the relationship between mothers and sons in fatherless families (e.g. Wallerstein and Kelly, 1980).

(v) *Feelings to do with home-making.* This group of feelings tends to be of short-lived intensity and can take one or both of two basic forms. It can be expressed in terms of anxiety over tasks which one is unable to perform well. This is again a learning phenomenon and decreases with time, though the number of individual tasks which have to be learned may be considerable. There are also lone fathers, however, who persist in a belief that, like "mother love", there is a phenomenon customarily called a "woman's touch" which is always missing in the motherless family, however competent and tasteful the father might be in the home.

The short-term nature of most home-making-related feelings should not obscure the fact that learning to cook, shop, wash clothes and tidy efficiently can cause fathers a good deal of worry, and can lead at times to friction between fathers and children.

(vi) *Feelings directly related to the former spouse.* As has already been noted, most lone fathers find the process of structuring a new parenting and home-making role less arduous than that of negotiating the separation from a former spouse (O'Brien, 1980). This applies whether the new family unit is created by death or marital breakdown. For widowers the nature of these feelings has been well documented in the literature on bereavement and widowhood (Marris, 1958, 1974; Marsden, 1969; Parkes, 1972). In cases of marital breakdown the adjustment of fathers and children is linked to the spirit underpinning the relationship between the adult partners — aggression or conciliation.

A general theme running through this paper is that it is essential to put the position of the lone parent and his children into a more general context of family structure and process; in particular we need to move away from a language of *pathology* towards a language of *transition* or *adjustment*, accepting that such processes may involve both strengthening and weakening factors for any individual or family. Tolstoy wrote in *Anna Karenina*: "All happy families resemble each other, but each unhappy family is unhappy in its own way." To which we might add that happiness is not the prerogative of a particular type of family.

Rutter (1972) considers that when examining the difficulties and stresses caused by so-called "broken homes" one is dealing with *distortion* rather than disruption of relationships. Presumably distorted relationships can also exist within "normal" family units, and as Hess and Camara (1979) point out, it is often forgotten that some family processes in divided and intact families might be similar, and that many processes within divided and intact families may show a good deal of variability. Hess and Camara claim that many studies, particularly those which use analytic procedures grouping families by marital type, ignore these "between-group" similarities and "within-group" differences. It may be that the most crucial variable is simply relationships between family members, irrespective of family type.

Mendes (1979) suggests that the parenting functions adopted by lone parents tend to fall within one of five "lifestyle typologies". As they apply to lone fathers, these are:

(1) *Sole Executive*. This denotes a lone parent who is effectively the only adult responsible for the care of his children. Some of these "sole executives" may be, in Mendes' words "tyrannized" by the two-family model, and concerned to be both father and mother to their children. Others adopt the role of a contributing co-ordinator, inviting and applauding appropriate contributions from their children.

(2) *Auxiliary Parent*. This type of lone parent shares parenting responsibilities with an auxiliary (real) parent who does not live with the family and whose involvement may vary from considerable to minimal. This auxiliary parent, according to Mendes, may not actually have contact with the children. Thus, whilst children adjust emotionally and cognitively to the realities of a mother's death or disappearance, their mothers are classed as auxiliary parents within Mendes' definition.

(3) *Unrelated substitute*. This refers to a person close to the father but not related to him who may or may not live with the family.

(4) *Related substitute*. This category includes, for a lone father, any one of his female relations. It may also include children within the one-parent family who adopt a parental function.

(5) *Titular Parent*. The last group includes those lone parents who, whilst having custody of their children are, for practical purposes, incapable of parenting them. Such parents include alcoholics, drug addicts and other parents in name only.

Children of Lone Fathers

Unfortunately, space does not permit us to examine the evidence on the effect of lone fatherhood on children. Suffice it to say that studies on children in one-parent families have dealt almost exclusively with fatherless families (Wallerstein and Kelly, 1980; Hetherington, 1979; Hetherington *et al.*, 1979; Gardner, 1976).

Two general points are worthy of our attention, however. Firstly, the transition to one-parent family status involves a renegotiation of intrafamilial roles, usually towards a less authoritarian and more democratic model (see e.g. Weiss, 1979). Secondly, age and experiential differences between parent and children, and between children of different ages, can lead to an incongruity of perception or reaction between different members of a family (Todres, 1975). To the extent that problems exist or recur between a lone parent and his or her child (Gardner, 1976), they need to be seen in the context of this process of re-negotiation and of the basic incongruity inherent in the intrafamilial environment.

Summary and Conclusions

In sum, then what can one conclude from this morass of evidence on lone fathers? Certainly, each father's position is a unique mixture of practical situations, a history of relationships and the father's own perceptions of his situation and efficacy. Certainly, too, research suggests uniformly that such difficulties as there are in the transition process are likely to be most intensely experienced in the first year.

Stresses to the extent that they exist are likely to be regular and unremitting. As George and Wilding (1972) put it:

> "One day of overwork and excessive worry is a common occurrence in the lives of most people. It is the cumulative effect of many such days with few prospects of any substantial ease-up that makes life hard to bear. This was the lot of many of our fathers."

It would be simplistic to suggest that lone fathers' reactions follow a predictable pattern whilst they adjust to their new status. This would ignore the complexities of the interplay between trauma and relief in the context of a past and continuing dynamic of relationships which are inherent in this particular process of transition. Thus, one should beware of making premature judgments on a lone father's adjustment or the family's functioning. Whereas many families might experience an initial period of practical and emotional confusion, others might continue to function perfectly adequately, perhaps with added strengths. Yet another group, perhaps motherless families with a lengthy history of conflict, might experience a tremendous sense of relief in their initial phase.

It is open to question how many of the adjustment problems which particular lone fathers experience could be alleviated by a mixture of public education and practical measures. Public education—in the sense of changing social attitudes—is a lengthy process and for the foreseeable future lone fathers will be faced with common misconceptions concerning their position and the prognosis for their families. On the other hand, it is highly probable that the psychological lot of many lone fathers would be improved if the major recommendations of the Finer Report were implemented. These concern:

(1) Changes in matrimonial law and its implementation, involving closer cooperation between legal and professional helping agencies;

(2) Improved financial arrangements for all one-parent families; and

(3) An increase in day-care provision, together with a greater flexibility in working hours.

Even with such reforms, however, attitudes of the community at large can often serve to isolate one-parent families, and Ferri's observations below often apply with particular force to motherless families, for and towards whom there are no ready conventions of behaviours:

"Far from being conducive to the reintegration of one-parent families into the social fabric, the ambivalent and often negative attitudes which society adopts toward such families seem only to isolate them and add to the multiple difficulties they face." (Ferri, 1976).

Although it can be said that there is nothing inherently pathological in the motherless family unit (Orthner and Lewis, 1979), there are risks which children in such families run. The child's adjustment is intimately connected with that of his or her father and the nature of the father's feelings towards his wife, his present role, and how the community views him. Furthermore, there is a delicate balance to be maintained between the family's need to restructure its members' roles and communication patterns and the child's basic developmental needs.

Failure to maintain this equilibrium can result in a basic distortion of relationships and affect the child's perceptions of the social world outside his home. At the same time, the process of adjustment may offer the child new opportunities to develop his or her functioning, capacities for social interaction and sense of responsibility (Weiss, 1979).

The evidence is uniform in suggesting that the first year is by far the most difficult period in the life of a one-parent family, with its complex and particularistic mixture of personal and institutional variables. The eleven factors below have been drawn from various pieces of research and are suggested as a guide to risk factors for both father and child in the one-parent family:

(1) The father was rarely involved in care-taking activities prior to becoming a single parent.
(2) The family is isolated from the father's extended family.
(3) The father has to give up work.
(4) The family suffers a sudden drop in its standard of living.
(5) The father is generally unwilling to re-allocate his time commitments in favour of his children.
(6) The father or child has no psychosocial outlet, or the father has no relief from full-time work and care-taking activities.
(7) The child has no regular, enduring and close contact with a female adult.
(8) The father is still in aggressive dispute with the mother, or is in a state of prolonged grief.
(9) The child is customarily used as the focus or outlet of parental feelings.
(10) Contact with the absent mother is irregular, or the issue of access remains unresolved or a source of conflict.
(11) Intrafamilial roles become distorted to the extent that the parent–child distinction is lost.

Essentially these form a kind of checklist which professionals working with lone fathers would do well to bear in mind when assessing whether a particular situation is potentially problematic. Linking these, and similar factors, to developmental patterns is the next step for research in the field of child-rearing by lone fathers. Until then, it is probable that many such men — and possibly their children — will suffer judgments based on assumptions rather than performance.

References

Ainsworth, M. D. S. (1979). Infant–mother attachment. *American Psychologist* **34**, 932–937.
Bain, C. (1973). Lone fathers: an unnoticed group. *Australian Social Welfare*, **3**, 14–17.
Barber, D. (Editor) (1975). *One Parent Families*. London: Davis-Poynter Teach Yourself Books.

Bowlby, J. (1953). *Child Care and the Growth of Love*. Harmondsworth, Middlesex: Pelican Books.

Brown, A. and Stones, C. (1979). A group for lone fathers. *Social Work Today* **10**, 10–13.

Brown, G. W. and Harris, T. (1978). *Social Origins of Depression: A Study of Psychiatric Disorder in Women*. London: Tavistock Publications.

Brown, R. (1980). Breaking Up: *A Practical Guide to Separation, Divorce and Coping on Your Own*. London: Arrow Books.

Chiriboga, D. A. and Cutler, L. (1977). Stress responses among divorcing men and women. *Journal of Divorce* **1**, 95–100.

Davenport, D. (1979). *One Parent Families: A Practical Guide to Coping*. London: Pan Books.

Douglas, J. W. B. (1970). Broken families and child behaviour. *Journal of the Royal College of Physicians* **4**, 203–210.

Douglas, J. W. B., Ross, J. M. and Simpson, H. R. (1968). *All Our Future*. London: Peter Davies.

Fasteau, M. F. (1976). *The Male Machine*. New York: McGraw Hill.

Ferri, E. (1973). Characteristics of motherless families. *British Journal of Social Work*, **3**, 91–100.

Ferri, E. (1976). *Growing Up in A One Parent Family*. Slough: National Foundation for Educational Research.

Ferri, E. and Robinson, H. (1976). *Coping Alone*. Slough: National Foundation for Educational Research.

Finer, M. (1974). *Report of the Committee on One-Parent Families*. Cmnd. 5629. London: HMSO.

Fraser, D. (1980). Divorce, Avon style. *Social Work Today*, **11**, 12–14.

Gardner, R. A. (1976). *Psychotherapy with Children of Divorce*. New York: Jason Aronson.

Gasser, R. D. and Taylor, C. M. (1976). Role adjustment of single parent fathers with dependent children. *The Family Coordinator*, **25**, 397–401.

George, V. and Wilding, P. (1972). *Motherless Families*. London: Routledge and Kegan Paul.

Goldstein, J., Freud, A. and Solnit, A. J. (1974). *Beyond the Best Interests of The Child*. New York: Free Press.

Greenberg, J. B. (1979). Single-parenting and intimacy: a comparison of fathers and mothers. *Alternative Lifestyles* **2**, 308–329.

Hansard (1980a). Written answers to parliamentary questions. *Hansard*, **984**, (176), Col. 551.

Hansard (1980b). Written answers to parliamentary questions. *Hansard*, **988**, (208), Col. 63–64.

Hess, R. D. and Camara, K. A. (1979). Post-divorce family relationships as mediating factors in the consequences of divorce for children. *Journal of Social Issues*, **35**, 79–96.

Hetherington, E. M. (1979). Divorce: a child's perspective. *American Psychologist* **34**, 851–858.

Hetherington, E. M., Cox, M. and Cox, R. (1976). Divorced fathers. *The Family Coordinator*, **25**, 417–428.

Hetherington, E. M., Cox, M. and Cox, R. (1979). Play and social interaction in children following divorce. *Journal of Social Issues*, **35**, 26–49.

Hipgrave, A. G. (1978). *When The Mother is Gone: Profile Studies of 16 Lone Fathers with Pre-School Children*. Unpublished M.A. Thesis, Child Development Research Unit, Nottingham University.

Keshet, H. F. and Rosenthal, K. M. (1978a). Fathering after marital separation. *Social Work*, **23**, 11–18.

Keshet, H. F. and Rosenthal, K. M. (1978b). Single-parent fathers: a new study. *Children Today*, **7**, 13–20.

Leete, R. (1978). One-parent families: numbers and characteristics. *Population Trends*, **13**, 4–9. London: HMSO.

Levine, J. A. (1976). *Who will Raise the Children?* Philadelphia: Lippincott.

Maidment, S. (1980). Child custody: unfair to fathers? *The Times*, 9th April, p. 7.

Marris, P. (1958). *Widows and Their Families*. London: Routledge and Kegan Paul.

Marris, P. (1974). *Loss and Change*. London: Routledge and Kegan Paul.

Marsden, D. (1969). *Mothers Alone: Poverty and the Fatherless Family*. Harmondsworth, Middlesex: Allen Lane.

Mendes, H. A. (1976a). Single fatherhood. *Social Work*, **21**, 308–313.

Mendes, H. A. (1976b). Single fathers. *The Family Coordinator*, **25**, 439–444.

Mendes, H. A. (1979). Single-parent families — a typology of lifestyles. *Social Work*, **24**, 193–200.

Murch, M. (1973). The motherless families project. *British Journal of Social Work*, **3**, 365–76.

Newson, J. and Newson, E. (1963). *Patterns of Infant Care*. London: Allen and Unwin.

Newson, J. and Newson, E. (1968). *Four Years Old in an Urban Community*. London: Allen and Unwin.

O'Brien, M. (1978). *Father Role and Male Sex Role After Marital Separation: Men Coping with Single Parenthood*. Paper presented at the British Psychological Society, Social Psychology Section conference, September 1978, U.W.I.S.T., Cardiff.

O'Brien, M. (1980). Lone fathers: transition from married to separated state. *Journal of Comparative Family Studies*, **XI**, 115–127.

Office of Population Censuses and Surveys (1978). One-parent families 1971–1976. *OPCS Monitor*. Reference FM2 78/2. London: Office of Population Censuses and Surveys.

Orthner, D. K., Brown, T., and Ferguson, D. (1976). Single parent fatherhood: an emerging family lifestyle. *The Family Coordinator*, **25**, 429–437.

Orthner, D. K. and Lewis, K. (1979). Evidence of single father competence. *Family Law Quarterly*, **13**, 27–47.

Parkes, C. M. (1972). *Bereavement: Studies of Grief in Adult Life*. London: Tavistock Publications.

Rutter, M. (1972). *Maternal Deprivation Reassessed*. Harmondsworth, Middlesex: Penguin Books.

Sanctuary, G. and Whitehead, C. (1970). *Divorce and After*. London: Victor Gollancz.

Santrock, J. W. and Warshak, R. A. (1979). Father custody and social development in boys and girls. *Journal of Social Issues*, **35**, 112–125.

Schaffer, R. (1977). *Mothering*. London: Fontana Books.

Schlesinger, B. (1978). Single parent fathers: a review. *Children Today*, **7**, 12–18.

Todres, R. (1975). Motherless families. *Canadian Welfare*, **51**, 11–13.

Wallerstein, J. S. and Kelly, J. B. (1980). *Surviving the Breakup*. New York: Basic Books.

Weiss, R. S. (1979). Growing up a little faster: the experience of growing up in a single parent household. *Journal of Social Issues*, **35**, 97–111.

Professional Intervention
in the Parenting Process

DOUGLAS HOOPER

Department of Social Administration,
University of Hull, Hull, England

In Mervyn Peake's fantastical novel "Titus Groan"(1946) he has Lady Groan say these words shortly after her new baby is born:

> "I would like to see the boy when he is six. Find a wet nurse from the Outer Dwellings . . . Call him Titus. Go away and leave the door six inches open".

A not uncommon fate for upper class children of an earlier era — and at least unequivocal. What it does in a vivid way is to remind the modern reader that parental discontinuity in one form or another is a practice of considerable antiquity. Discontinuities in a child's experience of parenting have probably always occurred in some form or another for many centuries, but what has obviously changed is the family type in which these discontinuities existed. The type described is (fortunately) a far cry from most contemporary families as far as child care is concerned. Stone (1979) characterizes — or perhaps caricatures — the present family as one which is an

> ". . . intensely self-centred, inwardly-turned, emotionally bonded, sexually liberated, child-oriented family type"

for which, with the historian's long view, he predicts no necessary permanence. Except, that is, for one aspect of this late-twentieth century family which is the growing concern for the children. He describes this concern as the only steady linear change in family arrangements over the last four hundred years. But again we should beware lest we ascribe our own particular value system to even *this* change, since he adds that as this concern for children has grown continuously, it has also oscillated between both the permissive and the repressive over the whole period of his study. He is not primarily concerned with the nineteenth and twentieth centuries; if he had been, he might well have documented another astonishing change in alternative parenting of all kinds with a marked swing away from co-operative or servant patterns to patterns of professional roles of many kinds.

This paper is concerned with these current roles, and attempts to chart some of the current issues and problems in a relatively uncharted area. Many kinds of professional action in families are now so common as to go unremarked, and yet the dimensions involved are still ill-recognized. The modern description for many of these actions is intervention, and although for some the term is pejorative (especially since it seems antagonistic to client self-determination) it seems justified here since the professional is often involved in precisely that act. A crude definition would be that intervention in parenting is any act on the part of a family outsider which attempts to alter, or to substitute for, processes in the child–adult system which would normally be carried out by the child's natural parents. The term "natural" then needs some definition here, and for the present purposes it would include adoptive and other forms of parenting which are so permanent as to be regarded as "natural". So defined, it is important to see that this pre-supposes no necessary biological linkage. Thus defined, intervention can be a wide variety of acts which range from the very circumscribed and isolated, to the all-pervasive and near-continuous parenting which takes place in residential settings.

Put like this, forms of intervention in parenting have probably always been present in society, although they have been discharged in very different ideological guises. For the last thirty years one would be forgiven for thinking that the only proper parenting pattern is that in which a very few children were cared for by an adult man and woman who were themselves in some sort of permanent relationship. It needs something like the Group for the Advancement in Psychiatry's Report (1973) to remind the modern professional that:

> "experience of parenthood is not essential for the successful growth and development of an individual to maturity. The experience of parenthood . . . may even be deterrent to self-development in some individuals . . ."

There is increasing evidence that in fact this particular family structure may fast be becoming the pattern for the minority rather than the majority of families at least in the U.S. and the U.K. (Rapoport *et al.*, 1977). One-parent families have been particularly studied in this respect and obviously many such parents manage the task of lone parenting very successfully indeed. Yet the expectation of being two parents in one is a considerable concern of the adults concerned, and a recent study showed that three quarters of the single mothers and half the fathers found the question of the second parental role a problem — indeed the authors describe it as, in their view, a daunting task (Ferri and Robinson, 1976). Perhaps eventually our society will come to accept that a single parent can often provide very adequate parenting provided he or she has adequate resources and support. But until that is widely acceptable such families will presumably absorb a good deal of the professional energy described here.

Intervention Systems

A number of structures exist which provide what may be described as benign interventions. Basically these are professional interventions which are actively sought by parents in the ordinary developmental cycle of the family to generally enhance total family functioning as they perceive it. A number of examples come to mind amongst which are the actions of obstetricians, midwives, health visitors, school teachers and the lowly child-minders. Perhaps the most powerful of these is the boarding school which can often create collective parenting for the children involved. There are those who would certainly not regard these experiences as "benign", but nevertheless the act on the part of the parents in selecting this form of experience for children is usually positive rather than negative. The other important observations on this type of intervention are that it is not normally substitutive, but complementary to already effective parenting. Finally the major temporal characteristic of this type of intervention is that it is always episodic and often transitional.

The second set of structures provided by professionals and semi-professionals offers what can be described as deficit interventions. Ordinarily because of some failure or lack, the parent(s) may either seek such intervention, or in some cases may have such an intervention thrust upon them by a concerned community. In these latter cases the professional's task is made doubly difficult by the forced nature of the intervention, so that neither parent nor child would use the word "parenting" to describe the professional behaviour despite that being actually the intention of the person concerned. For some children the intervention may not now be episodic and interim, but may be a complete alternative to the "natural" family structure. Yet ideologically most professionals insist that such measures should be seen as transitional even though the evidence suggests otherwise. One important intervention here occurs when children are hospitalized. It is only too well known now that such forms of intervention are often malevolent because they actually ignore the fact that they *are* interventions in the parenting process, and that the child involved is often in great need of substitute parenting. The problem really arose because the nurses and doctors both denied the sick child their own professional parenting and prevented the natural parents from continuing to look after the child as best they might. This is changing, but is still not entirely satisfactory (Hall and Stacey, 1979).

Having now discriminated somewhat crudely between the types of intervention which are offered by professionals, it would be as well to examine the actual size of the populations involved. Occasional intervention is almost impossible to estimate, but various studies through the recent years have "guestimated" that perhaps 10% of families will require parental deficit intervention of some quite specific kind (e.g. Wedge and Prosser, 1973; Department of Health and Social Security, 1976). Benign intervention (if one includes school) is obviously ubiquitous. Most research on the effect of the school on development has been concerned with the rather narrow areas of intellectual development. But many schools and especially those in "deprived" areas have taken on an increasingly explicit parenting task with some children. The effectiveness of this intervention is in doubt at the moment, although most of the available work is summarized by Rutter *et al.* (1979).

Within the deficit category there are about 100,000 children in the care of a local authority at any one time of whom about 40 per cent are in the care of foster families of some kind. The incidence of all forms of formal care has been found in the recent 16-year follow-up of the National Child Development study to be 3.7 per cent of their sample (Fogelman, 1976). This, the authors say, is likely to be a slight underestimate because of the slightly skewed pattern of their sample. Although we have almost no comparative data for previous periods these data further suggest that taking all forms of natural mothering and fathering into account, some 98 per cent of children are mothered and 92.5 per cent of children are fathered. These figures are, perhaps, a necessary corrective to some of the commonly prevailing views that children are widely un-parented. If the National Child Development Study accurately reflects the situation in the community at large, then the major part of deficit parenting will be concerned with intact family situations where skills are lacking, or not effectively deployed. Only perhaps 4,000 children a year actually need the community to find them alternative and perhaps permanent parents (CCETSW, 1978).

Parenting

So far in this paper we have successfully avoided defining the term in the title of "parenting". This is a relatively new word in the professional jargon. The reason for preferring it over child-rearing is that it defines an interactive process between adults and children and also lacks what to this writer are the overtones of animal husbandry! It also has other functions, since it adds to the meagre vocabulary of terms we have to describe such an important human activity. It discriminates the process of being a parent from parenthood on the one hand (i.e. the *status* of being a parent) and parentcraft on the other hand which generally refers to those skills, styles and attitudes which relate specifically to fulfilling the parental role. Obviously within the parenting concept mothering and fathering must also be distinguished. But here the aim is to maintain the focus on the generic term.

Fortunately knowledge of effective parenting is now accruing rapidly so it is possible to describe with some certainty the broad dimensions involved. There are obviously two sides to this social process as recent writers have sharply reminded us (e.g. Rapoport *et al.*, 1977) and we know a good deal more at present about the child's side of the relationship. Most professional intervention is carried out for the children's benefit after all! There are a number of statements in this area which may help us, since by studying them we should be clearer what form an intervention should take. Some are quite simple such as that of Kellmer Pringle when she says that children need parents who love them, the principal feature of this love being that the child is valued unconditionally and for his own sake and that this unconditional affection is communicated to him in all their relations with him (Pringle, 1975). She further adds that the child needs these loving parents to provide security, new experiences, praise and recognition, and the chance to take personal responsibility. This she contrasts with the child in residential care whom she describes as having no reliable past and no predictable future. Other workers have skirted the issue of parental love, but otherwise say similar things. In various places Rutter has listed the following important characteristics: 1. An emotional bond and relationship. 2. Secure physical base.

3. Adequate behavioural and attitudinal models. 4. Adequate control of behaviour. 5. An effective and established communication network (Rutter and Madge, 1976). Commitment and continuity are implicit in this list but not explicitly stated.

Surrogate parenting by professionals can obviously provide most of these conditions, and much professional activity is simply focused on specific parental deficits and increasingly in a much more active style than previously. These and similar approaches are sharply different from the older child-care tradition of intervention which often seemed to be more concerned with parent substitution either in part or in whole, and in which the child was the recipient of the inadequate care of the parents. The new approaches are ideologically much more technical. Both the examples given stem from an examination of the system properties of the parent–child group. But they do have certain limitations because they often focus on limited segments of the parenting, and also limit the intervention in time. Surrogate parenting in the active stance which is often taken by professionals working with these new models may well not be able to handle the longer-term parenting process. Nevertheless it is a useful and important corrective to the more passive approaches.

At the extreme end of intervention is residential care in which for some children surrogation becomes substitution. Both Rowe (1977) and Parker (1971) point out that the major problem of such parenting is continuity and commitment. Rowe particularly points out that ordinary families provide commitment, individualization, continuity of perspective, and reciprocity of relationship — all of which are seemingly very difficult to provide in residential settings. Of course the worst aspects of residential care have on the whole been recognized and corrected, particularly the undoubted knowledge that large communal units are the antithesis of any form of parenting. Yet even within this changed and small-scale model, there are still serious deficiencies. Berry (1975) in her study of the residential life of children showed that of the 44 institutional settings which she studied, 40 per cent of them involving nearly 400 children did not provide even a moderate degree of parenting on her measures. It should come as no surprise that the poorer units were associated with poor morale on the part of the staff, an important part of which was that they had inadequate support for the stresses in their work. Yet stress and inadequate support must be precisely two of the factors which led to breakdown of natural parenting in the first place! Although there is great need to be aware of such deficiencies, it is equally unreal for a wider public to expect unrealistically high levels of parenting which could probably only be matched by a very small proportion of intact families in the community. Many residential settings do take in very difficult children indeed, and substitute parenting can be very burdensome indeed. A vivid recent account of some of the stresses involved is given by Dharamsi *et al.* (1979) in their account of work in a children's home.

One especially pervasive problem is that of the degree to which such full-time care is transitional so that the children are intended to return to their own families sooner or later. It may well be that the most important aspect of the intervention which safeguards the natural parents' position is that the surrogate parent(s) sees herself as a "therapist". This is an unpopular position in a number of places now, but this may be because of the inappropriateness of the older psycho-dynamic models on which many of the earlier therapeutic ideas were based (e.g. Hazel, 1976). The major advantage of a therapeutic approach as compared with a caring approach is that there are generally specific goals for change which are set by the professionals involved and which they try to achieve. Thus the role of the substitute parents is much more explicit and can be evaluated. Yet there remains a very real professional problem which even the therapeutic stance has difficulty in overcoming. It is that as soon as the "professional" parents start trying to create the conditions of long-term commitment and so on, the professional then becomes increasingly engaged as a rival parent rather than a surrogate. In one of the few accounts so far of the children's own experience of these circumstances Timms (1973) gives an account of a child who had been "taught to hate her mum". Yet there is some evidence at least (Prosser, 1978) that children can manage two sets of parental relationships quite adequately. Although this paper has excluded fostering from consideration, these problems obviously arise acutely there. Several workers have shown quite clearly that not more than 5–10% of the children are in touch with their own families in contradiction of a theoretical ideology of rehabilitation (e.g. George, 1970; Shaw *et al.*, 1975).

Education for Professional Intervention

In the light of this evaluation of the issues involved, one obvious area for action is that of educating the young professionals. Tizard and Rees (1975) summarize this neatly when they suggest that the professional worker has to be free to plan so that the parenting impulses necessary to good work can be brought into play in a professional manner. But this is not enough. Any intervention requires the establishment of a novel social structure (albeit of a temporary kind) which provides for the additional presence of the professional worker and in its most complex form provides for residential care workers, field or clinic workers and natural family to relate together. Of course even to see this as a "system" is to take an important step forward in that the elements then become capable of analysis as well as action. As in almost all training for professional caring relationships, the early part of this education is towards making interactions often feel *un*-natural as they become the object of analysis and comment. But as these skills are acquired, they become more habitual and sequenced so that a more natural flow to these surrogate relationships is restored. These complex skills are not, perhaps, necessary for all those who may work with families but surely they do need to be a resource which is at least available to all so that good practice can be as widespread as possible.

At a time when family structure is becoming much less rigid, and more families disintegrate and reform we must expect that professional intervention will need to become very much better than it is at present. There is now no shortage of knowledge at least in some areas of parenting. The task is to develop innovative and imaginative ways of applying it.

References

Berry, J. (1975). *Daily Experiences in Residential Life: A Study of Children and Their Care-Givers*. London: Routledge and Kegan Paul.

Central Council for the Education and Training of Social Workers (1978). *Good Enough Parenting*. London: CCETSW.

Department of Health and Social Security (1976). *Fit for the Future*. The Report of the Committee on Child Health Services. London: HMSO.

Dharamsi, F. *et al.* (1979). *Caring for Children*. Ilkley: Owen Wells.

Ferri, E. and Robinson, H. (1976). *Coping Alone*. Slough: National Foundation for Educational Research.

Fogelman, K. (Editor) (1976). *Britain's Sixteen-Year-Olds*. London: National Children's Bureau Publications.

George, V. (1970). *Foster Care: Theory and Practice*. London: Routledge and Kegan Paul.

Group for the Advancement of Psychiatry (1973). *The Joys and Sorrows of Parenthood*. New York: Scribner.

Hall, D. and Stacey, M. (Editors) (1979). *Beyond Separation: Further Studies of Children in Hospital*. London: Routledge and Kegan Paul.

Hazel, N. (1976). Child placement policy: some European comparisons. *British Journal of Social Work*, **6**, 315–326.

Parker, R. A. (1971). *Planning for Deprived Children*. London: National Children's Homes.

Peake, M. (1946). *Titus Groan*. London: Eyre and Spottiswoode.

Pringle, M. K. (1975). *The Needs of Children*. London: Hutchinson.

Prosser, H. (1978). *Perspectives on Foster Care*. (See Abstracts and Annotations by R. Thorpe). Slough: National Foundation for Educational Research.

Rapoport, R., Rapoport, R. N. and Strelitz, Z. (1977). *Fathers, Mothers and Others: Towards New Alliances*. London: Routledge and Kegan Paul.

Rowe, J. (1977). In *Challenge of Child Abuse*. Edited by A. W. Franklin. London: Academic Press.

Rutter, M., Maughan, B., Mortimore, P. and Ouston, J. (1979). *Fifteen Thousand Hours: Secondary Schools and Their Effects on Children*. London: Open Books.

Rutter, M. L. and Madge, N. (1976). *Cycles of Disadvantage*. London: Heinemann.

Shaw, M., Lebens, R. and Cosh, A. (1975). *Children Between Families*. Leicester: Leicester University School of Social Work.

Stone, L. (1979). *The Family, Sex and Marriage in England 1500–1800*. Revised Edition. Harmondsworth, Middlesex: Penguin Books.

Timms, N. (Editor) (1973). *The Receiving End: Consumer Accounts of Social Help for Children*. London: Routledge and Kegan Paul.

Tizard, B. and Rees, J. (1975). Effect of early institutional rearing on the behaviour problems and affectional relationships of four-year-old children. *Journal of Child Psychology and Psychiatry*, **16**, 61–73.

Wedge, P. and Prosser, N. (1973). *Born to Fail?* London: Arrow Books.

Subject Index